How to Write Successful Business and Management Essays

How to Write Successful Business and Management Essays

Patrick Tissington

Markus Hasel

Jane Matthiesen

Los Angeles | London | New Delhi
Singapore | Washington DC

First published 2009
Reprinted 2009

SAGE Publications Ltd
1 Oliver's Yard
55 City Road
London EC1Y 1SP

SAGE Publications Inc.
2455 Teller Road
Thousand Oaks, California 91320

SAGE Publications India Pvt Ltd
B 1/I 1 Mohan Cooperative Industrial Area
Mathura Road, Post Bag 7
New Delhi 110 044

SAGE Publications Asia-Pacific Pte Ltd
33 Pekin Street #02-01
Far East Square
Singapore 048763

Library of Congress Control Number: 2008936815

British Library Cataloguing in Publication data

A catalogue record for this book is available from the
British Library

ISBN 978-1-84787-590-7
ISBN 978-1-84787-591-4 (pbk)

Typeset by C&M Digitals (P) Ltd, Chennai, India
Printed in Great Britain by the MPG Books Group
Printed on paper from sustainable resources

Summary of Contents

Contents

Contents

Foreword

When I was at my old-fashioned (but very good) state grammar school school in the north of England, we were coached in essay writing. This was in addition to my well-meaning teachers trying to help me understand all kinds of other things with varying degrees of success. I have to confess that I was not a good student at school but I did have two real skills by the time I left: an ability to saw wood in a straight line and a basic understanding of what an essay is. Fast forward twenty-five years and, as a lecturer, I find that few if any students have the latter skill (probably also not the former – but that is a different book!) so I set out to find a suitable textbook to recommend. There are quite a number available but I found many of them made essay writing more obscure rather than less so. I also found that often they were aimed at such a wide range of students they would use examples from subjects I didn't study (from French literature to medieval history), which added to my confusion. The logic behind writing this book was to provide a core text which students taking degrees in business schools could have access to – a dedicated text that (a) told them how to write essays in straightforward language and (b) used examples which they would find relevant.

This book has its origins in a module I teach at Aston Business School (Introduction to Organisational Behaviour) where I first began to realise that students were arriving at university without the skill of essay writing. About nine hundred students a year experience this module and I am grateful to them for their forbearance in acting as unwitting guinea pigs for this book. With such a large number of students, I have been extremely fortunate to have had the assistance of first Jane Matthiesen and, more recently, Markus Hasel to act as tutors on the course. They have taken the lead in supporting students as they struggled to work out how to answer the essays I set and between us we have formulated ideas about how students could be taught essay writing alongside the module content. This book is a team effort.

Our aim is to provide a single source text for all business students looking at essays for the first time. We hope the book will be particularly useful for first year undergraduates, as well as for those who realise later in their university career that they need to find out more about essay writing. We also hope that those starting postgraduate business courses – possibly from outside the UK – will also find the book of value. To those of you who are trying to fathom the intricacies of essay writing and whose first language is not English, I am in awe of your abilities – and, by the way, neither Markus nor Jane is a native English speaker so they completely understand the challenges you face!

Patrick Tissington
August 2008

Introduction

The driving force and idea for this book came from Patrick Tissington's experience on entering university for the first time aged 29 with an academic record which (a) dated from 10 years previously, (b) was science/maths orientated and so didn't involve writing essays and (c) was extremely poor (he was a late developer!) Markus and Jane were both educated overseas and found they had to come up to speed very quickly with the rather quirky nature of essay writing in UK universities – and for them English wasn't their first language so they very much empathise with overseas students who have the additional language burden as well as the challenge of decoding the rules of essays.

It is our experience that many students find essay writing difficult and do not even know where to start. While there are books on writing, none is specific to the business student and, though some contain very helpful information, having examples derived from English literature or sociology or history sometimes gets in the way of understanding rather than helping. So this book is intended to be specifically for business students and by this we mean students on any taught degree programme and include (among many others) undergraduates and postgraduates in general business and management subjects, specific degrees in marketing, human resource management, accounting, economics, operations, systems, consultancy, decision making and, of course, lots of similar degrees. Students on psychology, sociology, history, geography courses and so forth may also find it of help but the examples given will be more relevant to the former group.

What is an essay?

We have set out to explain what an essay is and what essay markers are looking for. The text is aimed at business students, both undergraduate and postgraduate, especially those who either haven't written for a while or perhaps have never been taught how to write essays. Also many overseas students are not familiar with essays in the form we use them in the UK so this is for them too.

How to use this book

The information in this text can be accessed in a variety of ways:

- you can read it all in one go

- you can work through it as you write your essay

- you can skim read it and come back to sections you find most useful.

For most students, the third option is most likely and indeed you should be able to skim through this book in an hour or two, which, considering the time you will be spending on writing essays, is a very sound investment of your time. To help with this we have included summaries, made the chapters fit the actual process of writing an essay (rather than the theory) and given examples to help you understand the steps. The book is intended to be useful for those who have either never been taught how to write an essay or those who have forgotten. In case some of you would like to progress beyond being able to write competent essays which will enable to you pass, we have included sections on advanced skills in Chapters 3, 4, 5 and 9 which you might like to come back to once you are happy you have got the basics right.

Chapter 1

An Introduction to Essay Writing

Chapter objectives

Having read this chapter you will:

- know what the book is about
- know how to use the book to your best advantage
- understand how to read books at university
- have planned which chapters to read in depth
- know what an essay is, why they are set and how to structure one
- know how to structure an argument using the SED format
- know what to look for in an essay question.

It is our experience that many students find essay writing difficult and do not even know where to start. While there are books on writing, none is specific to the business student and many contain helpful information that is lost or confused amid examples which may seem irrelevant to a business course. So this book is intended to be specifically for business students; by this we mean students on any taught degree programme and include (among many others) undergraduates and postgraduates in general business and management subjects, specific degrees in marketing, human resource management (HRM), accounting, economics, operations, systems, consultancy, decision making and other similar degree courses. Students of psychology, sociology, history, geography and so forth may also find it useful but the examples given will be more relevant to the former group.

How to use this book

- You can skim read it and come back to sections you find most useful.

- You can work through it as you write your essay.

- You can read it all in one go.

For most students, the first option is the most likely one. Indeed, you should be able to skim through this book in an hour or two which, considering the time you will be spending on writing essays, is a very sound investmentof your time. To help with this we have included summaries, written the chapters to follow the actual process of writing an essay (rather than focusing on the theory) and have given examples to help you understand.

Key points to getting the most out of this book

It is essential to get used to preparing for essays by being organised. This may be something which comes naturally to you, in which case skim read the first part of Chapter 2. For everyone else, read Chapter 2 thoroughly first! The second part of Chapter 2 shows you how to plan your essay – we think practically everyone could benefit from reading this even if you are reasonably confident about writing essays.

Lectures are very different from classes at school and you are supposed to work in a very different way. If you already have experience of university or college, perhaps you could skim read Chapter 3. Those of you coming from school – perhaps even more especially good schools – will find that university lecturers do not give you the clear direction you are used to. If you are at all uncertain of the rules of the game, spend some time on Chapters 3 and 4.

Essays are written in a particular style, so if you are at all uncertain what this style is, pay attention to Chapter 5.

If you have trouble working out how to use references – and especially if you have never heard the term – spend some time getting to grips with the referencing styles described in Chapter 6. Students ask most questions about this and it is actually very simple once you get to grips with it. Even if you think you understand referencing, you should go over this chapter to refresh your memory and check to see whether or not you have been using referencing systems correctly in the past. Then you can test your skills in Chapter 7.

Students are often found to have plagiarised by accident but reading Chapter 8 will help you make sure you are never accused of this.

Essays are very commonly set in exams and, while the main idea is the same as for coursework essays, Chapter 9 gives specific advice for preparing and writing under exam conditions.

Finally, the Appendices contain examples you can refer to and check back later. Perhaps you might even start here, by looking at the examples of good and bad writing in Appendix 5.

How to read books at university

As with just about all the books you read at university, you should not think of starting at the beginning and reading through to the end. You should *use* this book rather than simply *read* it. By this we mean that you will probably have at least some idea about the advice contained in parts of the book and you can skim read these sections quickly. Other parts you might need to start from scratch, so these parts you should read differently. We recommend that you first skim read, then read through taking notes, then read your notes and dip into particular sections again. (We have given more information about how to use books in Chapter 3. It may seem strange that we should be telling you how to read but Patrick didn't realise how to do this until halfway through his university career, by which time he'd wasted hours and hours of time and become needlessly stressed.) However, don't think this sounds too daunting a task or that it is too time-consuming. We have deliberately pared the information down to what is really needed and the skills you are developing will save you time in the future and, of course, help you get the most out of your university degree – surely the aim of going in the first place!

So start by looking through the Index and see if there are any areas you recognise as being ones you are comfortable with or you might need to concentrate more on. Use the grid in Figure 1.1 as a tool to plan how you are going to use the book and record your progress.

	Skim read	Read/make notes	Read notes	Reread chapter	Understood
What on earth is an essay?					
Planning					
Note making					
Material					
Writing					
Introduction to references					
Plagiarism					
Writing essays in exams					
Motivation					
Appendices – examples					

Figure 1.1   Using this book

What is an essay?

At its simplest, an essay is a written answer to a set question. However, there are particular styles for the setting of essay questions and also styles that apply to the way you should answer them. In some ways it's a bit like crossword puzzles; having subject knowledge isn't enough – you also need to know the code used by the person writing the puzzle. In essay writing the rules are simpler, but without the basic knowledge you probably would not be able to produce a good answer. So here are the basics.

- You need to assume the reader has basic common-sense knowledge but not subject-specific knowledge.

- You must justify **Everything** you write – ideally by referring to scientifically accepted work but (occasionally) by use of examples.

- You are expected to demonstrate that you understand the theories you present by summarising them. Make sure you don't reproduce exactly what you read in a textbook as this will be plagiarism (see Chapter 8).

- You must always acknowledge where you get your justifications from – see Chapter 6 on references and Chapter 8 on plagiarism for more information.

Structure – the basics

There is a lot more about essay structure in Chapter 5 but we introduce the overall idea here so you understand how the essay is going to look when you have finished it. It is difficult to be precise about the exact length of each section since that will depend on the number of words you have been set to use and on the essay question set and how you approach it. However, the basic structure is not at all complicated and can be summarised as shown in Table 1.1.

Why are essays set?

The idea of an essay is that it both develops and tests – they are not set by lecturers to make students suffer. The act of preparing an essay in itself develops subject knowledge in the student but the finished piece of work is also a way for the lecturer to assess how much the student knows. In fact there is another layer to this too in that essays make you think logically (building logical arguments like in a debate) and critically (not just believing the statements made by people but finding out how they justify what they are claiming). So by writing essays you develop knowledge while becoming more logical and critical. These are

Table 1.1 Basic essay structure

Section	Description	Tips
Introduction	A general short opening statement (one or two sentences). An overview of what is going to be in the essay. How the question will be answered. Link to the first section. One (short) paragraph.	Make sure it isn't too long and don't spend too much time thinking about it and rewriting it. The introduction only needs to describe how you have decided to answer the question set and you could even write it last. Many times students get hung up on trying to get this right. If you are struggling to write the introduction, you probably haven't planned the essay properly. Make sure that you tell the reader what to expect in the main body of the essay. Check that what you say you are going to do will answer the question.
Main body	Several paragraphs. Each paragraph with self-contained arguments (see p. 8 for what an argument is and therefore this section should be done). Each paragraph will answer part of the question.	This is where you really earn your marks. Follow the outline given in the introduction. Each section should follow the SED format: **S**tatement of claim; **E**vidence; **D**iscussion/evaluation (this is discussed more fully below). Justify *everything* you write by use of references (see Chapters 6 and 7).
Conclusion	Short summary bringing together the arguments. Possibly assess the limitations of the arguments. Show how the question has been answered, in parts and as a whole. One or two paragraphs.	Summarise the points made in the order you have made them. Your conclusion must answer the question set – no more and no less. Make sure it matches what you set out in the introduction.

key skills you learn at university. We thought about what coursework to set for our students but we kept on returning to setting essays because of these benefits.

What an argument is and how to make one

One of the most frequent comments made by lecturers is the question: 'What is your argument here?' An argument in this sense does not involve shouting or throwing crockery, of course, but is based firmly in logic. The best way to understand this is to use the following simple SED format in your writing.

- *Statement of claim*   You write what you are going to prove. On its own, a statement of claim has no value (i.e. it will not gain you marks). If you provide evidence for it, and then discuss and evaluate what it means, you are earning marks.

- *Evidence*   Relevant evidence would be scientific papers from peer-reviewed journals or textbooks (see Chapter 4).

- *Discussion/evaluation*   The evidence for and against your claim is weighed up and you show that your claim is justified.

Each paragraph should have this structure to it so each element is worthy of a little more description. See the following example paragraph illustrating this structure.

We can see from the collapse of Enron how dangerous pure intelligence can be as a predictor of achievement.[1] Enron started selecting employees solely on their intelligence test results so those who scored high on the tests were selected over individuals with knowledge and experience (Fincham & Rhodes, 2005). Senior managers encouraged these new inexperienced employees to explore new ideas and exploit new markets believing that intelligence was more important than experience. One psychologist claims that Enron's major mistake was believing and telling the young professionals that they were 'gifted' simply because of their high test results (Fincham & Rhodes, 2000, p. 145).[2] This led to the arrogance of the firm and they had they thought they could 'do anything' and 'jump into any market' (Fox, 2003, p. 145). This led to reckless decisions being made and was a major factor in the downfall of the company.[3]

Key: 1   Statement of claim

2   Evidence

3   Discussion/evaluation

Types of essay questions

Essay questions vary considerably between topics and between lecturers but in broad terms there are four basic types of essay questions. Each of these is actually asking you to produce a different type of answer. However, in answering any of these question types, you should always use the SED format.

Discuss

In this type of essay, you are frequently given a statement (often contentious) followed by the word 'discuss' – for example, 'Taylorism is still a relevant model to leverage performance gains in the workplace. Discuss.'
   To answer this question you would start out by describing what Taylorism is, then perhaps evaluate the features against literature or studies which contradict the idea that it does lead to gains. You might then return to the theory and extract any points which still have relevance.

Describe

The question here asks you to provide information about a particular topic but does not ask you to evaluate this. It is very unlikely you will be asked only to describe something, although this might be just part of a question as many essay questions have multiple parts. It is vital to make sure you note how many parts there are to a question and ensure you answer all of the parts. So a question might be: 'Describe the Taylorist approach to productivity.'

Compare and contrast

This format is very popular and you need to find the similarities and differences between two things to produce a successful answer. You should look to find equal numbers of similarity and difference and come to some sort of conclusion. If no conclusion is specifically asked for, just bring the essay to a close with a summary of the similarities and differences.

Evaluate

This is rather like the 'compare and contrast' question but the examiner has given you more latitude in how to go about answering the question. You don't particularly need to give equal numbers of points for and against, but the custom is that you give both sides of the argument regardless of what you feel the evidence shows. So you need to find something to say on each side. You are usually asked to come to some sort of conclusion and justify this through an evaluation of the evidence. Another favourite version of this question type is 'critically evaluate' which essentially means the same thing.

Combination essay questions

Some essays require you to do more than one thing. For example: '*Outline* the main organisational theories underpinning modern management and *discuss* their relevance to your professional area.' Clearly here you would need to describe the theories and then evaluate their relevance to your profession. If you only describe the theories, you are unlikely to pass. If you do not describe the theories sufficiently (perhaps you just name them), similarly you are very unlikely to pass.

Answer the question

The most frequently written comment on essays by markers is something to the effect of 'you have not answered the question set'. There are no marks awarded for answering a question the examiner did not set!
    Probably the most important advice in this whole book is:

1   **read the question**

2   **answer the question that has been set.**

Follow this advice and you are on the road to success! (There are more sample questions in Appendix 1 which are shown with explanations of how to go about answering them. You might like to use these for reference when you are first deciding how to answer the question you have been set.)

So, having looked at the basics, the next chapter moves on to how you go about the first stage of essay writing: planning.

Chapter 2

Planning

Chapter objectives

Having read this chapter you will:

- know the basics of how to plan your time
- understand the importance of keeping a diary
- understand the importance of planning your essay
- know what you need to do to plan an essay.

Have a plan. Follow the plan, and you'll be surprised how successful you can be. Most people don't have a plan. That's why it's easy to beat most folks.

(Paul 'Bear' Bryant, American football coach)

There are two sorts of plan you need to write an excellent essay: first you need to plan your time and, second, you need to write an essay plan. This chapter deals with these, starting with planning your time.

How much time do I need?

Sadly we can't give a hard and fast answer to this question. It all depends on a large number of factors but the key ones are:

- how much you already know about the topics you are writing about

- how quickly you read

- how focused you are when you are working.

But here's a rule of thumb passed on to us by a very experienced project manager:

- think of the absolute worst case for how long things take

- add a bit

- double it.

In other words, things will almost always take far longer than you think they will. You will almost certainly forget to factor in some key demands on your time. These demands will include a social life, sport, updating your Facebook page but also other essays, revising for exams and probably, these days, your part-time job. Be realistic about your own ability to concentrate and how tired you may be due to other things going on in your life. But do remember that you will need to allow enough time for this: think how long it takes you to read things – are you able to both read quickly and internalise the topics? Or is the essay topic one you haven't really got your head around yet? Our best recommendation is that you begin to plan as soon as you know there is an essay being set. This is known as starting with the end in mind – think ahead to the hand-in date and think what you want to have achieved by then. We also very strongly suggest that you plan backwards from the hand-in date by breaking down all the things you need to do – collect reading material, read, make notes, etc. and set yourself milestones (dates by which time particular tasks should be completed). Perhaps our strongest recommendation overall in this chapter is to get yourself organised. You need to be organised when you start work and many successful students treat university a bit like a job – by being organised. (This is going to be something you will find invaluable when you start work so get used to it now.)

Get organised

> Here's our checklist for being organised.
>
> 1 Get a diary.
>
> 2 Stick to your diary appointments (have it with you all the time).
>
> 3 Never agree to *any* appointments without looking in your diary.
>
> 4 Sort yourself out a good place to work.

1 Get a diary – electronic or paper

You absolutely have to have a diary so you can organise all the things you need to do at university, from meetings with tutors, lectures or hand-in dates to your social or sporting arrangements. You particularly need to record your essay milestones, noting what you need to have achieved by the dates you set yourself. In terms of format (electronic or paper), it is very much a matter of personal preference but do think that, in order for your diary to be any good, you do need to have it with you and you must refer to it constantly. We would say this probably means the online ones (e.g. those you get with Gmail or Hotmail) aren't much good since you could be asked to commit to an appointment when you aren't logged in anywhere or don't have a computer in front of you. However, you might have one built into your phone which you can synchronise with Microsoft Outlook or Entourage. This works well and there are lots of different PDAs too which are very reasonable. If you go for a paper diary, think of getting a filofax or something similar whereby you can add the diary as inserts and keep some notes and important addresses too.

Write all your appointments in your diary – it doesn't matter if they are to do with work or not. This will really help you build a realistic appreciation of what time you have available to devote to your course-work when you are planning.

2 Stick to your diary appointments (have it with you all the time)

Whatever format you use, make sure you stick to the appointments you make in it. You can only really do this if you have your diary with you pretty much all the time. At an absolute minimum you must have it with you in lectures (to note important hand-in dates, for example) and at work group meetings (note meetings and ensure you don't agree to do work which will interfere with your individual assignments). Also, if you have a part-time job, always take it to work with you so you can make sure you don't agree to work on days when you should be doing your university work. Take it with you when you go out in the evenings too – but that isn't to do with essay writing!

3 Never agree to *any* appointments without looking in your diary

Even if you think that you are free on a particular day, always say you need to check in your diary. As we have already said you should have your diary with you all the time but, if for some reason you don't, never be tempted to think you can remember all the things you have written in the diary. Do not agree even to a casual game of five-a-side football without checking your commitments for the day. Your friends may think this behaviour odd but you will find that most successful people are diary obsessed. Start now!

4 Sort yourself out a good place to work

Students work in all sorts of conditions but, in general, those who are successful will have spent some time really thinking about how to create a place to work. Yes you need to have eating and sleeping sorted out but, if you don't have a place where you can work productively, then you are limiting the return on the investment of time and money you (and often your parents) have put into your university career. Think of it as showing that you are serious about studying at university and work out where you will be able to work. It doesn't matter if you are in a hall of residence, a rented house or living with your parents, you need to have a quiet place to work. We recommend that you find a place which is for work alone. It doesn't matter if it is a small desk in your bedroom, clear everything else away from it and have the area just for work. If you really have to, you could decide to work only in the library. We don't recommend this for all your work, however. This is not because libraries are bad places to work, it's just we think you should be able to have your work left ready for when you need it. Perhaps you like having wall charts showing important dates or maybe you want to leave a certain book open, ready to start on the next day. However you do it, keep this space for work alone – a nice surface to work on, perhaps a space for your laptop or desktop computer, a bit of room to keep books, lots of blank paper and pens/pencils. You don't need a vast area, just a space that when you enter it you are thinking about your studies.

Finally something to avoid in your work space – being disturbed. If you find that your housemates are noisy, either find ways of controlling when they are noisy and work at different times or find another place to work. In extreme cases, even if you are having an absolute ball but you can't work, you really should think about moving somewhere else where you can work as well as party. Do not fool yourself that you can take your laptop to a coffee shop and do your work there. You really need to have more controlled work space than this. We have even seen students trying to work in noisy bars – they are fooling themselves if they think they are doing any valuable work. In our experience, the way to ensure you have a great time at university is to make sure you can work most efficiently at your studies so you have more time to have fun.

For example, it will really help the quality of your work if you actually finish writing a week before the deadline. What you can then do is put it to one side for a few days and then read it through and decide what changes (if any) to make. You will be surprised when you do this at how much good stuff you have written – but also how many blunders you have made which you can then correct. It really shows you know what you are doing when you hand in a piece of work which is error free. On the flip-side, imagine what the impression on the marker would be if there were typing errors or incorrect references in the first paragraph of your work. Even if things like spelling are not directly assessed, silly mistakes will definitely leave a poor impression on the marker, so pay attention to detail. Remember that academics actually get promoted on their ability to be picky so if you have made even a tiny mistake in the format of your references (see Chapter 6), punctuation or spelling, they will definitely spot it. So make sure you get all the little details right as well as the important big ideas.

So now you have got yourself organised, what are you going to do with the time? We have some rules of thumb which should help you here.

- Spend a fair amount of time reading and making notes.

- Spend more time than you think you should on the plan.

- Allow yourself time to do the writing.

But make sure you allocate time evenly – actually we think you should spend roughly equal amounts of time on each of the three parts. Since two of these parts are planning elements, this means we think you should spend more time planning than writing. It is perhaps one of the most frequently misunderstood things about essay writing so we're going to emphasise it by putting it another way: students would think they should spend more time writing than preparing whereas, to do well, you need to spend about twice as much time planning as writing. The reason for this is that, if you start to write without a very clear plan, your writing time will actually be spent planning on the hoof as well as writing. Obviously doing two things at once means you don't do either task all that well. Concentrate on planning first – and of course you can't really plan if you don't know the material, so that's where the reading and note making come in (see Chapters 3 and 4 for more information on these key skills).

To summarise, we would advocate the old army saying: 'Time spent in reconnaissance is seldom wasted'.

In simple terms, Figure 2.1 illustrates our recommended time allocation, which shows that you should allocate twice as much time to the preparation (two-thirds) as the writing (one-third). Actually, if you have prepared properly, the writing should be really straightforward.

The essay plan – focusing on the question

We are living in an era where we have access to more information than ever before through the Internet. Google and other search engines have made it fabulously easy to find information so we find that students are tempted to type in the key words from the question into the search engine and go from there – possibly paraphrasing the pages they find from the search. In Chapter 4 we will discuss what material is and is not

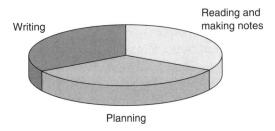

Figure 2.1   Essay writing – allocating time

acceptable. But at this stage, having read the previous paragraphs, you will be very much aware that you should not be doing any of the final writing yet. You must first formulate an essay plan. We touched on some of the features of a good plan in Chapter 1 but now we go into detail about what you need. (In Chapter 5 we will discuss how you use the plan to write the essay.)

We have seen that an essay consists of an overall structure of introduction, main body and conclusion. So your plan needs to contain notes about what these sections will contain. In fact, the introduction is something you should ignore for now. The reason for this is that you are going to build the ideas for how the essay will go and only once you have built this can you write the piece describing the story. When you come to do the actual writing the introduction can often be written last, so don't fall into the trap of trying to construct an introduction when you don't yet know what the main body is going to be. Many students make this error, believing that the writing should be done in the order it is read (see Chapter 5 for further discussion on this). In an era where students are now expected to word process all essays, there is a great temptation to search a topic on Google and start typing. This section will include advice on what sources are needed (with more detailed information in Chapter 4) and so what planning is required to ensure all the material is assembled before the essay is written.

Before you start to formulate the plan, however, it's useful quickly to remind you of what you are about to do. The idea of an academic essay is for you to show your lecturer how well you understand and evaluate the models and theories you have been taught on a specific topic. So it is, of course, essential that you understand the material. However, you then need to take a critical look at it all and come to a logical conclusion, which you reach by logical argument. Along the way, lecturers are also interested to see how you can organise your thoughts and present them clearly in writing. Most of all though, you *must* answer the question set and *only* the question set. A really common mistake is that students start off an essay in the right way but forget to answer parts of the question or even deviate onto a question of their own. So the first step in formulating your essay plan is to focus your attention really closely on the question. Your plan depends on your full and complete understanding of the question so you are setting out right from the start to answer the question set. This is one of the most important keys to you achieving good marks from the essay. The person marking will have a set of things they are looking for you to write and the clues for what these are will be set out in the question. If you don't do what you are asked, you really stand little chance of doing well.

So start by breaking up the question.

- Read the question over and over again.

- How many parts are there?

- Is one part more important than the others?

- Do you need to come to a conclusion?

- Do you need to compare and contrast?

- Do you need to critically evaluate?

- Write out the question (do not type it) in full in the middle of a sheet of paper.

- Draw arrows to the separate elements of the question – use highlighters if you like.

This process of analysing the question will enable you to start planning your essay. It makes you think about:

- what you already know which you can include in the essay

- what you will need to find out about

- whether or not there is a particular focus to the question

- the things you need to have in mind when you are reading.

The plan – an overview

Introduction

You don't need to think about the introduction yet. Ignore it for now and jot down notes for it when you have finished your reading.

Main body

This is the essence of your plan. Having read the question, write out some subheadings with a couple of bullet points with brief notes about what you might be going to say. Also make subheadings for theories you think you might want to include but don't know enough about yet. These should be your targets for reading.

Conclusion

You might be able to make some bullet points for this but don't worry if you can't think of a conclusion right away. You should draw your conclusions from the material you write and the arguments you produce along the way. You should have an idea where you are going to take your essay though if the question is asking you to come down in favour of or against something.

So now you have an overview of what planning involves. All the steps you have read about in this chapter will be explained in later chapters in more detail. Part of your planning process is to pick the most relevant issues and aspects. So there you go, if you want to know specifics about a particular step in getting your masterpiece on track, then jump straight to that section. Good luck planning!

Chapter 3

Reading and Making Notes

Chapter objectives

Having read this chapter you will know:

- the importance of reading the set text before lectures
- the stages of reading and note taking
- how to use mind maps to collate information
- what questions to have in mind in order to think critically about academic texts
- some important points about the use of technology.

Understanding academic writing can be tough – in fact students sometimes tell us that they can read a sentence and understand the individual meanings of every word in the sentence and yet have absolutely no idea what the whole sentence means. Don't worry if this also applies to you – it actually means you are normal! Academic writing is a particular style of English which on the one hand could be described as compact but on the other means it can be found to be unintelligible and because of this is sometimes called 'academese'. Just reading your textbook through once is unlikely to help you very much so we have broken the process down into steps for you. We find that if students approach academic reading in this deliberate way rather than just thinking 'normal' reading is enough, most of the time the understanding follows on.

You need to fully understand the topics you are going to be covering using this system before you start the essay because you need to have this knowledge before you start to plan your answer. Essays at university are not about just showing you understand an area, they are about showing you have *mastery* of them and can build logical arguments. This preparation work is designed to give you a good basis to start planning your essay. Incidentally these steps will also leave you better prepared for exams and other coursework too, so we recommend you get into the habit of doing this all the time you are at university. This process will help you get a lot more out of your course as a whole.

We approach reading and note making as being closely linked activities and recommend you follow the steps listed below which we will describe in detail.

- Make notes before lecture.
- Skim reading.
- Take notes during lecture.
- Review notes after lecture.
- Reread the text.
- Make notes for essay writing.
- Read smart.

Make notes before lecture

In order to get the best out of your lectures, you need to put in a little bit of preparation time. This need not take very long but will pay off in terms of your understanding the material better and quicker. Most lecturers these days will make their slides available to be printed off before the lecture (and if they don't – ask them!) Once you have printed them off, you have the basis for your notes on the topic – and with most of the information printed, you won't have to copy down loads of information during the lecture. If you have the option to choose a format for printing, we often find that having the slides three to a page is useful, as it leaves you room next to them to make notes of your own. So print your lecture slides well in advance of the lecture and find out what the relevant reading for the lecture is going to be.

Skim reading

You now need to spend a few minutes reading with your slide print-offs close at hand. The idea is for you to very quickly read through the material which is to be covered in the lecture and note down any key points you don't understand. You will always get better results if you arrive at lectures with at least some idea what the topic is, so that when you hear the models and theories presented by the lecturer it will not be for the first time. Reading before the lecture is probably the most important step for you to take on board from this section because experience tells us it is the step you are most likely to omit, but we also know that it is probably the most productive. If you have read the material first, you can then use the lecture to clarify the areas you don't understand and to reinforce the areas you are happier with. But don't worry about reading thoroughly – we are saying you should 'skim read' which is where you read through very quickly and don't stop when you don't understand something. Just the act of reading the words will actually be helping you to understand once the lecturer covers the area. You should not take very long over this and, as you become well practised, you might be able to do this in about 15 minutes or so – a very worthwhile investment of your time.

Take notes during lecture

Take your notes to the lecture and follow the points in the lecture on them. Make very short notes for things you now understand or for follow-up later on. It is really hard to listen and write at the same time, so try to keep your writing to much abbreviated note form rather than long sentences. You are going to look at the notes again straight after the lecture so you only need to remind yourself of things rather than write them out in full.

Review notes after lecture

Before you forget what you were thinking about in the lecture, go over your notes again. As long as you didn't have lots of things to follow up on, this shouldn't take too long but it is so important you make sure that you have understood the brief notes you made in the lecture and write any notes which are very brief in more full detail so you will remember them later. If you leave this for more than a couple of hours, you will forget – so make sure you do this before disappearing for coffee with friends.

Reread the text

Before the next lecture, you now need to sit down again and reread the set chapter. Again have your notes to hand so you can further build on them. This time you should read more slowly and thoroughly – but do skip sections which don't seem relevant to the course you are taking. This should take a bit longer than the first skim read but by now you should be fairly sure of the material. Make some attempt to understand sections you didn't follow until now but don't get hung up on them. If you are still stuck, make a note of what you don't understand and move on. You can ask for help on this by asking your fellow students, looking up other text-books on the topic (sometimes reading another author's description can really help) or contact your lecturer. Many courses these days use an online discussion board so try posting your question on that.

Make notes for essay writing

Now you have made notes on the topics, you need to move on to preparing for the essay. You will find that following the steps before this stage will make the process of planning and writing your essay so much easier. The next set of notes you need to make is the first step towards writing your essay. The first notes you need to make are concerning the essay question itself. As described in Chapter 1, questions often have more than one part to them so you should note what your answer needs to contain. Jot down some likely theory you could include – referring to your lecture notes to make sure you have included everything you are likely to need. Now go back to the text again. Read through again, but this time with the essay question in mind. Likely quotes should be noted with full references to enable their ease of use in the essay.

Read smart

It is a good idea to go beyond the set text – in fact many lecturers insist on it. Use the set reading as a starting point then follow up promising references and search using your library catalogue. Do not read whole books or, necessarily, complete academic papers: look at abstracts/summaries/introductions/conclusions to see if they are relevant. Focus on what you need to extract from the books and journals.

In our experience, lecturers will work from a chapter of a key text for each lecture which they publicise in advance of the lecture. If this information is not given out, contact the lecturer to find out what reading you should be doing. Be wary of very long reading lists – you can't be expected to read everything. Perhaps some of the references you are given are duplicates of similar sorts of books so don't feel you necessarily have to read all the set texts. If you have read a section and feel you have got a good understanding of the material, leave it at that.

While you are reading, think critically about what the author is saying. By this we mean you should get into the habit of having some key questions in mind when reading.

- What are the main findings?

- Has the author provided strong evidence to support claims?

- Have any other researchers pointed out particular weaknesses in the theory?

- Are you convinced by the arguments presented? If not, think of what logical argument you can present for saying you are not convinced.

- If you think the theory is strong, show why you think so.

- For each article or book you read, get into the habit of recording the information you will need for your reference list. In fact, you will save yourself a lot of time later if you actually record this in full in the format it will be needed in later (see Chapter 6 for full information on how to format references) i.e. author, date, title, publisher, place of publication. Some students use software to help them do this – the standard program is called EndNote but it isn't at all essential to use this as it is more for advanced researchers who have to organise hundreds of references.

A few very important points about technology ...

- It is probably best not to take a laptop into lectures. It might look like an easy way to take notes but in practice we find that students are tempted to do other things instead – we did a check once and out of twenty-five laptops open in the lecture, only three were being used to take notes and all the others were variously on Facebook or playing online games. If you are being distracted like this, you are not getting the most out of the lecture.

- Switch off your e-mail when writing – having e-mails pop up will interrupt your train of thought.

- Don't ever just start writing with a view to cutting and pasting – it can be actually much more difficult this way. Start with subheadings from your essay plan and start to fill in the paragraphs.

- Notes are much more useful if they are written by hand rather than typed. There is more flexibility this way too and you can easily carry round a few sheets of paper and have these next to the computer when you start to write.

- A very useful idea is to use a mind map – and don't think you need to be able to draw. Just a series of lines and bullet points are fine. We've included one we did when we were planning this book (see Figure 3.1 overleaf). Just by having information arranged on the page in this way helps you to take the information in at a glance. If you write in lists, you'll naturally start reading at the top of the page and read downwards whereas with a mind map you can take in more information at a glance. Try it for taking notes in lectures. You might also like to try a flow diagram when you are building a final picture of what your essay is going to cover. This is particularly useful when you are writing a long essay or dissertation as it means you can keep reminding yourself whereabouts you are in the 'story'.

- Keep copies of your work – you should make sure that you have at least one separate copy of your essay. Also beware of leaving memory sticks in university computers – our lost property office has literally dozens of them. Put your name and contact details on yours to be safe and think about keeping it on lanyard. One option is to e-mail copies of your work in progress to yourself so it is stored on a server as well as on your computer.

Advanced reading skills

The best way to get better at reading is to practice. There really isn't a short cut to the skill but investing time in this and other skills at an early stage will really pay dividends later on. We would recommend the following.

(Continued)

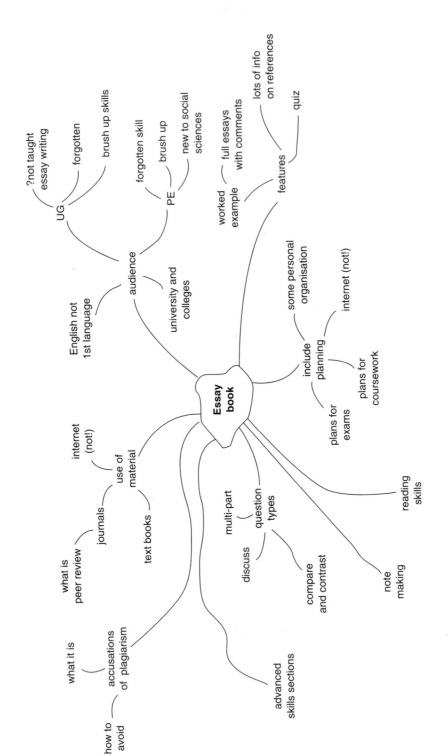

Figure 3.1 A mind map

(Continued)

- Become faster at reading.
- Targeting
  - read broad
  - read deep.

Become faster at reading

By the time you reach university, you will have already developed your own style and pace of reading. Some people naturally read faster than others but, regardless of how fast you read when you arrive at university, you will almost certainly benefit from learning how to make yourself read faster. There are specialist books and courses on speed reading and quite a number of websites devoted to the subject and, if you are really interested, perhaps you could break off now and have a go at these. In principle, the concept is to move from reading word by word (or even letter by letter) to scanning your eye across the page and gaining an overall sense of what material is there before focusing in to more precise (and slow) reading. If you have had the experience of showing your essay to an academic, you will find that many of them can take what appears to be a cursory look at your carefully crafted work and immediately tell you what you have and have not done. Academics are people who virtually read for a living so they have become used to it somehow. You need to learn it more deliberately as a skill. There is one exception; some people naturally skim read anyway and for them, perhaps they could do with learning how to read more slowly and deliberately – which is covered in the next section. Work towards being able to drift your eye down the middle of the page and avoid reading individual words. Can you get any sense of what the author is saying? Keep thinking about almost de-focusing your eye so you are not reading the words, just absorbing the overall message as if through some sort of sixth sense. Once you have established a vague idea what is in a section or chapter, you can decide whether or not you want to read it in more detail. See if you can get to a stage of reading more than a page in a minute – even for dense texts on large pages this is possible! The idea is that you can very quickly get to know whether you want to invest time in reading a chapter in detail or not. Once you have this skill, it will come in useful for the rest of your working life so the investment of time practicing it is well worth the effort.

Targeting

Now you are building an ability to read quickly, you have made it possible for you to read more in the same time so use this skill wisely by first reading broad and then deep.

(Continued)

(Continued)

Read broad   Most lecturers give reading lists to accompany their lectures. In fact many of them don't really expect students to read all the books they set as there are simply too many titles on the list. Patrick remembers being confronted with a reading list of about 20 books for just one module. Realising it was impossible to read all the books, he probably read none of them. A far better attitude would be to see how many of the books were available in the library and then at least get them off the shelf to have a glance at them in the library. Having used your speed-reading skills to get some sense of the value of the different books, you can then take out the ones you really think are going to be of use to you, and only those. With journal articles, you can pull these out online and look at the abstract and ask yourself whether it looks useful/interesting or not. Then you can download only the papers you think are going to help you.

Read deep   Having assembled the reading you think is going to be useful, now is the time to read deep. You still don't need to start from the beginning of a textbook nor do you even need to read complete research papers. Just focus in on the bits you think are going to be relevant then settle yourself in a comfortable place to read slowly. For those of you who naturally read quickly, this requires a conscious effort to slow down and read every single word. One useful way of slowing down is to read through once fairly quickly, then go back over the relevant sections taking notes. Which brings us neatly on to the next advanced tip on note taking.

Advanced note taking

There are different sorts of notes for you to be making – are you writing a coursework essay or revising for an exam? For the former, you need to be noting likely looking quotes from the text as you go along – but do make sure you record the place you are quoting from (paper or book), with page number. This means you can use the notes directly when writing your essay. Some people refer to this process as being a sort of treasure hunt where you are searching for nuggets of treasure which will help you answer the essay question. You should be ruthless in reading only the parts of the text which are going to help in your quest of writing the particular essay set. Even if other sections look interesting, perhaps make a note of them for reading another time. For exam revision, you are unlikely to be expected to give precise quotes so it is better to note down useful summaries of theories, write down author and date and the name of the theory if there is one. Try to work on short summaries as you work through the reading so when you come back to your notes you no longer need to read the text again as everything you need from it has been extracted.

Chapter 4
Material

Chapter objectives

Having read this chapter you will:

- understand how to use your set text.
- know what other resources you might need (journals – what they are and where to find them).
- know how to use your lecture notes.
- know not to use the Internet.

A word of warning before we start this chapter. It is vital to check with the lecturer what material is expected in the essay since this varies between universities, between courses and between lecturers. For example we tell students on our first year Introduction to Organisational Behaviour module that they only need source from the set text in order to pass the course but more material will be needed if they want a high mark – but many of our colleagues don't allow this and others are not so clear cut in setting the criteria in this way. So make sure the advice here is consistent with the conditions your lecturer sets. The use of notes will be further examined in terms of their use in forming the essay plan as well as ways to incorporate material from academic journals and other textbooks.

These days most modules will specify a set text for use on the module or perhaps a number of books. Often the information in the module outline (information available before you start) will include a chapter or chapters for each week of the module, together with a list of additional reading which might include journal articles as well. Students often ask what they should be doing with this information – for example, how much do I need to include in my essays? How can I read all the material in the list? You'll be pleased to know there are some simple answers.

The first thing to understand is that most lecturers provide a list of quite a number of books so that you have a choice and they do not in any way expect you to read them all. Perhaps the list includes a range of sources so you will have more of a chance of getting hold of it in the library or perhaps there are just a number of very similar texts available. For example, in one module we have taught (Introduction to Organisational Behaviour) there are quite literally dozens of excellent textbooks and they are extremely similar so if you read one, you wouldn't really gain anything by then reading the others. Lecturers will provide a comprehensive list to enable students to see that there is a range of material available – and possibly to show that they have done their preparation work! Frequently asked questions by students are along the following lines.

- How much do you need to cite?

- How many references do you need to have read?

- Can you just use the set text?

We have some answers to these questions but we would like to preface them by restating the health warning stated earlier – you should *always* refer to your university guidelines and regulations as well as specific information for the module you are studying and the advice of your lecturer in addition to the general rules of thumb given here. Our advice is based on our recent experience at a number of UK universities (both pre and post 1992) but your university may well have different ways of doing things.

For level one courses (i.e. first year undergraduate) we would suggest that you largely base your essay on the set text. Make sure that you completely understand the material in the set text relevant to your essay before adding anything else.

For level two courses (second year undergraduate) we recommend that you start with the set text and always include at least some other material – be it other books or journal articles.

For final year courses, we would expect that the lecturer would be providing quite a range of material and probably won't be steering you towards a single set text. At this stage we would expect the lecturer to be drawing your attention to the key themes and theories in an area, providing you with some clues as to the literature but then in general allowing you to find things out for yourself.

For postgraduate courses, we have often found that modules are actually more focused. You are asked to cover such a huge amount of ground on an MSc that the material is often presented for you and you might not have to go very far beyond that. You will of course need to understand the material extremely well and the lecturers at that level are looking for complete mastery of the theory and an advanced ability to think critically about it. You will be expected to follow key theories back to their original sources – this is often quite easy and looks great if you actually invest the effort to do it thoroughly.

Advanced skills – material

Ambitious students often ask about how they can go beyond a pass mark and go for a really high mark. Our advice always begins by asking them if they are 100 per cent completely sure they have got the basics in place. So, before you even consider going for additional material, here's a checklist:

Foundations checklist

Question read, reread and understood. ☐
Question broken down into constituent parts. ☐
Relevant material from module (lecture and set reading) reread and notes made. ☐
Answers to all parts of the question planned (using set material). ☐
Essay plan written. ☐

If you have honestly ticked all the boxes in the foundations checklist, then (and only then) can you start to look for additional material to include. The reason we lay down the law on this is because students sometimes try to go for the extra marks without making sure they have secured the basic marks. Sadly this means that they don't do well at all – even sometimes failing because the basic material is not understood and included. You must remember that, even though there is unlikely to be anything in the wording of the question which specifies what theories or other material you should include, there is an unwritten rule which is that the marker will expect you to use any relevant material from the lectures and set reading in your essay. The reason for this is partly logical and partly psychological. The logical part is that your lecturer has spent considerable time in deciding what to include on the course taking into account the level you are at, the course you are on, the expectations of the external examiner and so on. He or she has then spent even more time working out the wording of questions so as to test whether you have understood it or not. If this lecturer is presented with an essay which does not make full use of these resources *even if the essay answers the question set fully*, it is quite likely to receive a lower mark. The psychological part is that, if a lecturer is presented with an essay which contains little or no reference to material from their lectures, the assumption might well be that the student has not attended the lectures and may even lead to a suspicion that the essay is plagiarised with the thought, 'Why would a student go to all the trouble of finding different sources from those provided?' A further point to consider is to think of the basic information from the textbook and lecture as being the foundations whereas the additional material and extra work is more like ornamentation.

(Continued)

(Continued)

So, get the basics in place first before even considering the advanced sources. If you can tick all the boxes in the foundations checklist, now you can consider going beyond the basics.

So far as additional material is concerned, we would suggest the following:

- original sources

- academic papers

- other texts

- quality resources.

Original sources

Although institutions will have their own customs and practice about essay writing, most (in our experience) allow students in the first year to focus on a small number of sources. Progressively in further years you will be expected to go further beyond the core material presented in the lectures and most masters-level modules do require students to go to original sources.

By original sources, in general we mean that you go and read the actual theory rather than a summary of it in a general textbook. So, instead of using the 'cited in' reference style discussed in Chapter 6, you will be able to report that you have read the original paper. In other words, you most likely would take the reference from the textbook, find the book or paper it referred to in the library and read the relevant sections. You don't have to read the whole book or even the whole paper, just go back to the original source. Sometimes this can be quite a surprise and you may find that the summary in the textbook omits important information. Or you may also find that other distinguished scholars have made major criticisms of the work which might raise questions about the validity of the theory you can include in your essay (properly acknowledged, of course!). For example, if your essay included something about motivation, you might decide to include a section on Maslow's hierarchy of needs (most student essays on motivation do – it isn't necessarily a good idea to focus on Maslow in motivation essays but we are just giving you an example.). You could just refer to the summary in your general textbook using the 'cited in' format. However, you could go to your library and pull out the original work – in this case there are a number of original sources but you might look at the first paper in which the theory was put forward, which was Maslow 1943, or maybe the book, which is Maslow 1954. The difference in the text is small (see Chapter 6 on exactly how to cite this and all other references) but you are show-ing that you have actually gone back to the original work, have read it and are citing direct from the horse's mouth so to speak. In some cases, the original work may be rather difficult to understand at first but in many cases there isn't anything to be afraid of. Actually this is one reason why the Maslow example is a good one because the origi-nal paper is extremely easy to understand and is a very good read.

You will receive extra marks for doing this as you are showing that you can follow a line of enquiry yourself and that you have worked out how to find original sources and have the knowledge to be able to read and understand them.

A word of warning: be extremely wary of claiming that you have read something when you have only read someone else's summary of it. Often published work in the social sciences has several interpretations and the person summarising it might even have some things wrong. For example, we have had examples of students making extravagant claims for the material they have read but we noticed that some of the papers they claim to have read were written in languages the students didn't speak! This sort of exaggeration of one's reading can in fact lead to accusations of plagiarism in some cases (see Chapter 8 for full infor-mation about what plagiarism is and how to avoid doing it). So make sure you cite only the sources you have really read.

Academic papers

There are many oddities in the strange world of the university lecturer and perhaps oddest of all is the academic paper. Students don't usu-ally realise that lecturers in research-led universities actually get pro-moted almost exclusively on the basis of the research they publish not on how well they teach. In fact most lecturers would consider that teaching is less than half of their job – and for professors it is even less. Carrying out research of itself though does not create knowledge – it only creates it in one person's head – so it needs to be shared. Also, research needs to be scrutinised to make sure the conclusions reached are valid. So, what happens is that when you carry out a piece of research, you write it up and submit it to a journal where it is reviewed by experts in that field and, if accepted, is printed in the jour-nal. These journals are not the sort of thing you see in the newsagents but to academics are highly prized places to have your name in print.

These 'peer reviewed' journals are by and large the source for the material you see in your textbooks and referred to by the lecturer as this process of review is the means by which research is either accepted as being 'scientifically' valid or otherwise. Some of the top journals will

(Continued)

(Continued)

reject as many as 90 per cent of the papers submitted to them which is meant to show that the papers they do accept are of extremely high quality. So, these are great places to cite from and if you find a recent paper on the topic of your essay, it can be a great way of showing that you are up to date. Your library will have access to a very large number of journals via its electronic databases so you'll need to find out how to access them. You will probably have been told how to do this in your induction week but you are equally likely to have forgotten! In our experience, librarians are very willing to help students so long as you are polite and you don't ask them to do your work for you.

Other sources

You will have been given set reading for the module so, as discussed earlier in this chapter, you should make sure you first understand this. Then a good way to go further is to follow up on key references within that set text. By key references we mean the ones which are used a lot or on which the set text relies. Having read these sources, you then can follow up on the references used in these – and so on, more or less ad infinitum. These days all good journals are available online so you should have access to a huge range of material. Be careful not to be too ambitious as you could become side-tracked into seeking out all manner of obscure references. Also, not all the books referred to will be available in your library. Most libraries have some system of inter-library loans for students but we would generally recommend you avoid doing this too much as it takes a vast amount of time and you will almost certainly be able to get as good (or better) material from the library – if it isn't in stock, it is really very likely that you don't need it!

Additional resources you might consider are those published by reliable sources perhaps on the Internet. Before you reach for Google, however, a very stern word of warning. Be very careful indeed about what information you cite from the Internet. For example, citing information from Wikipedia is a fairly sure fire way to fail our course. Wikipedia is great, but the information on it is completely unchecked so cannot be regarded as a reliable source. Also, easy to understand definitions perhaps placed on the web by consultants is also a very poor resource. Some examples of good Internet sources might be government information published on their own websites (statistics, reports, policies), White Papers published by reputable professional bodies (for example the Institute of Chartered Accountants in England and Wales, the Chartered Institute of Personnel and Development, Confederation of British Industry). Our general rule is that students must not cite from the Internet, but at this advanced level, you are completely free to do so – as long as you ensure you are using reputable sources.

Quality resources

Finally a more general word on the quality of resources. Just because something has been printed and made into a book does not mean to say it is a valid source. In general terms you should look at the qualifications of the author and the quality of the publisher to see whether you are reading a reputable source or not. A hard and fast rule is to avoid self-published books and those written by non-academics. In the same way that not all books have the same value, so too for academic journals. Not all journals require the same level of scholarship and many have a very low barrier for publication. The top journals have a pretty ruthless sifting system which means that you really can trust papers published in them. A good way to work out which journals you can cite is to get an idea about how they are rated by other academics. At Aston Business School we publish a list of journals and how we rate them on our website. (Other institutions do the same thing.) So if you are in doubt about the quality of the journal, have a look at the rankings before you even start to read any papers.

Finally, if you really want to show dedication, you could see which academics are the leading researchers in the field and you could contact them direct to see if they have any new work which is about to be published. There is a pretty considerable time lag between a paper being accepted and it appearing in the public domain so most academics will have list of 'in press' papers. They might not want you to cite such work or let you see it but it might be worth a go. Again, do not waste time on this or rely on a leading academic to answer your essay question for you. You absolutely should not write them an e-mail asking 'Do you have any ideas on this?' or 'Could you give me a clue how you would answer this question?' Any replies you receive may not be polite! If you are particularly interested in a topic and perhaps are thinking about taking your studies further in that area (e.g. studying for a PhD in the field), it is fine to contact leading scholars and you may be pleasantly surprised by how approachable many of them are. Almost all academics have their e-mail address on their institution's website so they aren't hard to contact. Beware of citing work which is so up to date your lecturer hasn't read it – making your marker feel stupid isn't a good idea!

References

Maslow, A.H. (1943) 'A theory of human motivation', *Psychological Review*, 50: 370–96.
Maslow, A.H. (1954) *Motivation and Personality*. New York: Harper.

Chapter 5

Writing Essays – Marmite on Paper?

Chapter objectives

Having read this chapter you will:

- know the difference between essays at university and those at school
- understand in detail the structure and format of the essay (building on Chapter 1)
- know what an essay plan is and its importance
- know how to plan the actual writing of your essay (building on Chapters 3 and 4)
- have a checklist for the entire essay project.

Are essays similar to Marmite? Well, it seems to us that you either love essays or loathe them – just like Marmite! Perhaps it is closer to the truth to say that some students seem to be good at writing essays while others really hate it. For the latter group, it is very often simply down to them not feeling confident enough – they assume they are not very good at it and, low and behold, this becomes true. We also find that essay writing can become a very stressful part of university life and students dread the whole process. There is a concept called self-efficacy in psychology. It is the belief that you will succeed in whatever you are doing pretty much regardless of what it is. Of course, self-efficacy can be increased by learning and knowing more and developing particular skills, but it can also be a general state of mind. The military is very good at building this which they do by progressively putting recruits through more and more difficult tasks – each of which the recruits think they can't do. Having been shown time and time again that they can actually do things they initially thought they couldn't, eventually they believe that they can do pretty much anything they want. In some senses university life is the intellectual equivalent of this. University accepts you at a particular academic level and, by presenting you with an escalating set of challenges, increases not only your knowledge but also your belief that you can overcome intellectual challenges in a general sense.

We often find that in some ways taking the first step in writing an essay is perhaps the most difficult. Students sometimes stare at a blank computer screen and don't know how to start. Naturally this has a pretty awful effect on their confidence. But also if you ask for help from a lecturer, there isn't much we can do to help if you have nothing to show us. So having confidence is really important to enable you to get started in the first place and then to keep going when you begin to doubt that you can do it. So for all of you who fear the thought of having to write an essay, it is time to raise your self-efficacy. For all of you who are confident at writing academic essays – not to be confused with school essays – this might be a good refresher, clarify particulars you might not be entirely sure of or give you new ideas about how to approach essay writing in the future and be even more efficient.

We hope that, by following the steps laid out in this book, you will have been able to arrive at the point where you are able to at least get going on your essay and this chapter is where the actual writing begins. It is quite deliberate that this chapter comes well into the book rather than at the beginning – you don't start actually writing an essay until all the preparation has been done. If you try to start writing too early – you will find it is indeed hard work. However, if you have done all the work in note making, planning and organising yourself, the actual writing – if not easy – will be straightforward. Indeed we think that if you are finding the actual writing too difficult, the problem will have been caused by shortcuts you have tried to make in the earlier stages. So make sure you have all the various pieces in place before you begin the writing. Before you go any further ask yourself whether you have got a detailed essay plan including:

- a plan of what your arguments are going to be

- outlines of SED sections

- outline of overall essay

- notes covering all the topics you need.

If not, you should go back to those sections in the book and get them in place before you carry on.

Academic versus school essays

If you happen to be in your first year at university while reading this, then this might come as quite a surprise to you. Academic essays are not like essays you wrote in school. As you will see in the next chapter, academic essays are all about references which acknowledge that the statements, findings and theories you are using in your essay are not your own work, but someone else's. (You will read all you need to know on the topic of references and how to make them correctly in Chapter 6 and in the Appendices of this book.) In general terms, essays at school were there to show that you had knowledge of an area and you were encouraged to report in detail theories and studies. An academic essay requires you to write in a very coherent, structured way and the key is that you must develop logical ways using evidence. The basic idea is contained in Chapter 1 of this book where we described the SED format. If you didn't read this first, you perhaps should flick back to it and have a look at what we mean by SED. While you are there, also refresh your memory about the basic structure of an essay. As this book is targeted specifically at business students, let us use a business example.

Imagine you are supposed to write about the economic impact of changes in the demographic structure among the population. A lot of Western countries are facing the huge problem that their so-called baby boomers (people born during the birth boom in the years following World War II) are about to retire or have retired already. This means that, within the next years, companies and economies as a whole are facing a huge shortage of workers, in particular skilled workers (like all of you reading this – yes you are the skilled workers companies and other organisations are looking for and will be doing so increasingly in the future!) When at school you were writing a lot more general essays, not really using a significant amount of references (if any), showing your knowledge to the teacher and generally making sure to get as much information in as possible to show how much preparation you had done. An academic essay, however, is not just a list of knowledge, it is a coherent argument. Instead of simply writing a few paragraphs on the subject showing the different aspects and issues you have read and learned about, it is now about making sense of them. You now need to analyse the relevance, relationships and connections between the different aspects and weigh up the pros and cons. You are doing nothing less than telling a coherent story where your individual arguments making up the whole are supported by evidence from the literature. It is important, however, that your story is a selection of relevant, important things. Do not ramble. Make sure that you have chosen those important aspects, supported by evidence, nicely wrapped in a good coherent story. Your story has a beginning, a main body and an end: the introduction, the main body with all your evidence and the conclusion (a summary and analysis of your evidence).

So here is a quick checklist to see if you are writing academically.

- Is it a coherent story?
- Are individual arguments supported by evidence?
- Do you have three parts: introduction, main body and conclusion?

Planning your essay

We have looked at the differences between a school and an academic essay. Let us now shift our attention to how you go about writing an essay. First, never just start writing an essay. Always start with planning it. Before doing this, however, make sure you understand exactly what you are asked to write about – make sure you understand the essay question. There are always some students who have written a really good essay, but simply on the wrong subjects or are slightly missing the point. No matter how good the essay would be theoretically, it is at worst a fail and at best a low mark. So make sure you get the initial stage right. Once you have done this, you are likely to start reading through the literature to see what others say on the subject. What needs to be done for the reading phase is described in detail in Chapter 2 and is introduced in Chapter 1. Also you might like to go back to Chapter 3 to see how you should be making notes and how to do it efficiently and to Chapter 4 to see what material you need to include. If you are happy that you know how to make notes in the right way and you have got all your information together, you are now able to start with your essay plan.

The first step to take is to draw a general outline of what you think should go into the question. Scribble down different ideas on a piece of paper and move them around until you think the order is all right. In other words, write down topics that you think will need to be included in your essay and which will make up the content of your essay (see Figure 5.1). You are likely to rearrange the items at some point, but the important thing is that you start to give yourself an idea of where your essay is going. But let us go through it so you can produce a plan or map leading you to a successful, easily written essay getting you those great marks you are heading for.

Important note

We are showing here how to write your essay *plan*. Most universities discourage the use of subheadings and bullet points in essays and you should check with your lecturer before using them in an essay. Indeed many universities also forbid the use of diagrams and most will frown on the use of pictures. Our advice is to check but if you are in any doubt, just use straight prose with none of these features.

> Overall outline
>   Subheadings
>
>   • Bullet points
>   o List references according to place in essay so the essay
>   can be written in a flow.

Figure 5.1   General format to use for your essay plan

We are assuming that you have done all your preparation, reading and scribbling down some ideas. The next steps will then be as follows (see also the example plan in Figure 5.2).

1 Rearrange the topics you want to discuss in your essay. All you need at this point is to simply write down headings as you would use in your essay.

2 Below your headings write down all the subheadings, that is the top-ics, aspects, theories and findings you think are relevant. What you want to do at this point is not to write down who exactly said what, but again subheadings to remind you what to write in your essay.

Essay plan

Essay question: Analyse the economic impacts due to demographic changes in the UK population.

Intro

I recommend not to focus too much on planning your introduction. Your introduction can either be written after you have written your main body or before. It is likely that you will benefit if you not only use the introduction as telling the reader where you are planning to go with your essay but also use it as an additional map guiding you through your essay writing.

Main body

1) Demographic changes

    1.1) Ageing of population >fewer skilled workers
National statistics Ageing age structure
1.3) Migration
National statistics International migration
1.4) Immigration
National statistics IMPS (immigration etc.)
1.5) Available workforce now and in the future
National statistics Population estimates, population trends
National statistics GDP growth estimates time series data

2) Requirements by organizations

    2.1) Skilled workers
British chamber of commerce migration value Anderton (1999)
2.2) Increasingly university-educated staff
Anderton (1999) Hijzen (2005)
2.3) Flexible workers
Segal (1995) Castells (2000)

(Continued)

Figure 5.2   Essay plan
Source: This is an actual essay plan used by Hasel when an undergraduate. Obviously he chose one which delivered a good mark!

(Continued)

---

3) Economic impact

    3.1) Shortage of workers
National statistics Population trends British chamber migration value
3.2) Loss in productivity
Haskel & Martin (1993)
3.3) Loss in export contracts
Temple (2002)
3.4) GDP loss
National statistics GDP

4) Political counteractions

    4.1) Greater focus immigration selection
British chamber immigration Home Office
4.2) Greater focus on bringing more people into university
DfES

5) Organizational counteractions

    5.1) Greater use of workforces formerly not involved as much
(e.g., women, older employees)
Panteli (1999)
5.2) Greater use of in-house trainings
Buick (1997) HBR
5.3) More flexible work arrangements to attract good people
HBR Kim (1981)
5.4) Greater use of incentives to attract and keep good people
Boston Consulting
5.5) Better starting salaries
Prospects

Conclusion
Don't need much here as you are really summing up and drawing conclusions from what you have written and argued.

---

3 At this stage write down who said what. If you want to make it even easier for yourself, write down the page number. This will help you in quickly finding your resources again. When you first start doing this type of planning it will seem like a lot of work, but believe me, it is worth it. Not only will it make writing very easy as you only have to follow the map in front of you, but you can use it as a checklist to see whether you have included all these important aspects you think should be part of your essay.

4 Now it is time to start writing.

As you see in Figure 5.2, the easiest way is to make a list. You don't really need an outline for the conclusion as an essay develops and you will see what best comprises your conclusion once the introduction and your main body have been written.

For each part, list what you want to say, in which order, and list who said what (i.e., the source you have read it in) next to it. You can also put down the page number so you can find the section you are referencing again quicker. Try also to put them into an order so all you have to do when writing your essay is to follow the outline you have created. Look upon the outline as a map which guides you from start to finish.

Writing your essay

With your great essay plan before you, it is now time to harvest the benefits of all the preparation work. The order in which you write your essay is really up to you. Whether you want to write your introduction first and then your main body, or your main body first and then your introduction, is really your choice. Both have advantages, but opting for the latter will allow you to build up a mental map of where you are heading. By no means, however, write your conclusion before anything else. Your conclusion should always come last; you will see why in a bit. Two final pieces of advice, which a lot of students are not aware of:

DO NOT USE YOUR OWN OPINION ANYWHERE BUT THE CONCLUSION

And

EVEN THEN IT MUST BE COMPLETELY JUSTIFIED BY EVIDENCE IN THE ESSAY

Let us now look what goes into which part and how much detail is needed to write this excellent piece (see Figure 5.3 for a general guideline and template).

Your introduction

An introduction is the part of anything explaining to the reader, listener or learner where you are going and what they can expect. When writing your introduction keep in mind your reader who wants to know on which journey you are taking him or her. It is, therefore, the part stating the background information, mentioning the core aspects of your essay and the importance of why you are writing this essay and the reason why you have chosen those specific variables you are using to explain, analyse or discuss the essay question. Let us use the example in Figure 5.3 again: your introduction to answering the set question on demographics and their economic impact will most likely tell the reader about the ageing of society leading to economic impacts, including the impact it has on the job market. It will also have a brief section on the importance of discussing this change and on the area of the economy you have chosen to analyse. You should

(1) Introduction leading into
(2) Main body

- Concepts explained.
- Concepts argued in relation to each other.
- What do findings show?
- Where will it possibly go?

(3) Conclusion

- Your conclusion should round/sum up what you have explained throughout your essay
- You need to conclude your arguments
  - Show the indications, implications and future possibilities

Let's say you have a 1500-word essay to write, then spend up to 300 words on the introduction, approximately 1000 words on the main body and up to 300 words on the conclusion. So you see your main focus is the main body of the essay. Do not make the mistake of writing a one-page introduction or conclusion. We see a great many students 'spending' too many words on the introduction and conclusion sections. See Chapter 1 to remind you of the basic structure.

Figure 5.3   Structure you should use to write a good essay

then tell the reader which parts of the demographics and the economy you will be focusing on. You would, therefore, have an introduction looking like this (as they say in films, in order of appearance).

1 *First few sentences:* Background information (such as size of economy, changes in market).

2 *Next few sentences:* A brief mention of the ageing problem.

3 *Next few sentences:* A brief mention of its impacts and importance of discussing this specific topic.

4 *Final few sentences:* The variables you have chosen leading into your main body.

We mentioned at the beginning of this section that an introduction is an indication of what to expect. When you learn something new you usually get an introduction. You remember the first time you opened your mp3 player? It had a manual, did it not? Your introduction is the manual, telling the reader what to expect when reading your product, your essay. In terms of length of your introduction, you can see in Figure 5.3 the advice is to spend no more than about 300 words on your introduction when writing a 1500-word essay. This obviously changes depending on the length of your essay, but as a general rule of thumb, never spend more than about one-fifth of your word limit on your introduction and conclusion.

Your main body

As you can see in Figure 5.3, your task is now to explain the concepts. In our example, you will now go through your essay plan (remember it is your map guiding you through your essay) and follow the structure you have chosen. Again in order of appearance for our example in Figure 5.2.

1 The first thing we want to do is to inform the reader about the demographic changes that have taken place, what we can expect from population movements and what future predictions regarding workforce and population say and how they are likely to impact on our employee resources.

2 The second part of your essay should talk about what is required by organisations. What type of labour do they need to stay competitive or to survive in the UK? What have people said is available and what does the modern organisation expect from its employees? Some of the literature states that people need to be more flexible to survive in today's working environment. Now with an ageing workforce this may become more difficult due to people's desire to stay with their families, lack of language skills or simply because of physical constraints such as the inability to travel a lot.

3 Our third part is now looking at the economic impact the ageing has with regards to the economic and organisational requirements. In our example, it is now that you really start getting into the analysing part, linking the different aspects together. We have spoken about the demographic changes and organisational requirements. We now need to discuss how the interrelationship affects the economy, the way organisations can do business, the impact it has on worker availablility and productivity and the overall economy. But we can also look at the opportunities arising for those skilled workers due to the shortage of them organisations face.

4 According to our plan, our fourth part will deal with political actions taken to counteract the problems created through the demographic change. The important thing is that you link the different sections into each other. You do not simply list the different things you have read. You analyse them in context. The story you are telling now focuses on what governments do and which regulations may positively or negatively affect the economic impact.

5 Your fifth and final part of your main body should follow your plan and discuss what companies do and are able to do to counteract the current and future problems. You discuss the relative value of incentives offered to potential and existing employees to recruit and keep them. The important point is again that you do not simply list them, but view them in the context of your previous discussion and the aspects you have highlighted. For instance, remember we want to analyse what economic impacts the demographic changes have and therefore need to see how the workers' demands and skills impact the way organisations organise their human resource strategies.

Your conclusion

What makes a good conclusion? We have found that a great many students think they have great conclusions but, when they get their essays back, are amazed to see that they have been criticised for what they have included (or not included). First of all, do not introduce any new concepts, findings or theories in your conclusion. If you want to discuss particular aspects, do so in your main body. Your conclusion is a summary of what you have written and a place for discussion. You are now able, for the first time, to offer your own opinion in the light of what you have analysed or explained. In our example you might now want to say that the demographic changes regarding the age development in the UK and the increasing importance of highly skilled workers for UK business can be seen as a big threat to the economy. However, by looking at the strategies developed and implemented by both the government and business, this impact may possibly be minimised. You may, also at this stage, give your own opinion. For instance you could highlight one strategy you consider, from what the evidence is showing, the most effective at counteracting the negative effects for the UK economy. You could also say at this point whether you think governmental policies are more important than business strategies in controlling negative effects or vice versa. You could also say that only a combination of the two is likely to lead to optimal success. The conclusion is yours.

The wrap up

Finally finished. You spend days and nights writing, drinking a lot of coffee and tea, and have now finally written the last sentence. What to do now? Just hand it in, right? NO! Please do not hand in your first draft. Something happens while you are writing down your own words; you cannot see the wood for the trees. In other words, what you think is a masterpiece needs to be read again. You might have spelling errors, unfinished sentences or incoherent parts. But don't worry, for now you are finished and do not have to deal with your essay again. Take one or two days off before proofreading your essay. If you think why wait to proofread, then here is a good reason: you have developed tunnel vision. Reading your own piece of work straight away only leaves you thinking that it is a masterpiece. By walking away from it for a couple of days, you gain the necessary distance, allowing you to read your essay more objectively.

Review your essay in light of the recommended stages, listed below.

1 Read the essay question thoroughly.

2 Make sure you entirely understand what you were asked to do.

3 Read the relevant literature.

4 Make notes on the literature.

5 Make an essay plan (headings).

6 Add subheadings (topics and authors).

7 Give the essay plan a detailed structure (notes).

8 Start writing. Start with the introduction, then your main body and finally your conclusion.

9 Check if everything is there.

10 Leave it for two or three days.

11 After two or three days proofread it.

It is now that you are able to decide on the quality of your essay. Make sure your essay matches your essay plan, answers the question set (all parts of it), the spelling is correct, references are all there, your reference list is complete (for references see Chapter 6) and your arguments tell a good coherent story. We have designed a checklist to help you (see below).

Writing checklist

Use this list as a working document as you write your essay to check that you have covered all the bases. Especially make sure you don't lose marks at the last minute because you can't find references or you have used the wrong format.

Fundamentals	✓
• Number of words	
• Font size	
• Spacing	
• Referencing style	
• Named or anonymous	
• Hand-in date	
• Hand-in location	
• Submit electronically	
• Any other specific instructions for this essay?	

Planning	
• Note hand-in date in your diary.	
• Look to see what other coursework you have.	
• What other events have you planned (e.g. holidays, sports tours).	
• Is there a choice of questions?.	
• Draft essay plan (headings, subheadings, bullet points of notes).	
• Initial reading (set texts).	
• Initial reading (lecture notes).	
• Collect material – other texts, original work, academic journals.	
Writing	
• Check correct layout (line spacing, font type, font size, referencing).	
• Type out the question in full at the top of the page (so you can refer to it frequently to make sure you are answering it).	
• Type out headings, subheadings and bullet points from plan.	
• Work through filling in the detail to each.	
• At the end, reread the introduction (does it match the question set and your conclusion?).	
• Check for spelling and grammar.	
A week before hand-in	
• Put to one side for at least a day.	
• Reread checking against set question.	
• Ask a friend to read it.	

• Make amendments.	
• Check references.	
• Check referencing style.	
• Check spelling/typos.	
A day before hand-in	
• Re-check hand-in requirements.	
• Last read through checking references and typos.	
• Print out and put in a folder somewhere safe ready for hand-in (perhaps put in your bag by the door ready just to pick up).	
Hand-in day	
• Check you have essay before leaving.	
• Leave earlier than usual (allow extra time).	
• Hand it in.	

If you can tick all these boxes, then – but only then – hand in your essay and you are much more likely to get this great mark your masterpiece deserves. Unless you have missed answering the question, but we are sure after reading this book you will be fine and know what to look out for. Once you have all done this, you should no longer be a hater but a lover of essays – you see, just like Marmite.

Advanced writing skills

Only once you have achieved all the points up to the week before hand-in date in the Writing checklist should you think about going beyond the basics. The checklist, if followed correctly with the right material and argument, is easily sufficient for a really good mark. If you want to go beyond a good mark, then we suggest the following additional checklist which we will expand on below.

Writing style – does it flow?	
Nailing the argument.	
Have you gone beyond just answering the question?	
Read and commented on line by line by someone else?	
Set aside and reread?	

Writing style

Often markers will talk about whether an essay 'flows' or not. Essays which do not flow might achieve a reasonable grade but if you are shooting for a good first, you really need to make sure you are able to write in a flowing style. The good news is that the concepts here are fairly straightforward. The bad news is that putting them into action effectively does take time, experience – and patience. Explaining specifically what flow looks like is not all that precise but it is a combination of some key elements. The most basic of these is that the reader must be aware of what is coming next and where the writer is taking you. This is where essay writing differs from other sorts of writing where surprising the reader is part of the game (novels, for example). In an essay, the reader must be told precisely what is going to happen in the next section and then be led through these points in the order promised. If you are going to make three points, tell the reader this is what you intend doing. Otherwise after the second point we will start to wonder how many more there are! This is a point made in the notes on the sample essays so you can see some examples of it being done quite well and others where it has not been. Look for the difference in how you experience reading the essay when it doesn't have sufficient signposts. Our experience is that you start to feel lost and wonder where the student is going – the conclusion being that if a marker doesn't understand whereabouts the essay is going, the belief is that the student didn't understand either. In terms of advanced skills, the requirement is for absolute clarity so the reader knows what is coming up and, low and behold, it all is delivered. In a way it is like great pop music – the first time you hear a great song, it seems like you have heard it before. This is flow.

Nailing the argument

Of course any essay worth a pass mark must have to some extent answered the question set. For advanced skills this is true too, but

(Continued)

(Continued)

of course you now need to answer all parts of the question completely. Often we find that students have probably done so but it hasn't been made absolutely clear what the argument is and how it has been evidenced. Do not assume the marker will understand what you meant. Actually state clearly and unambiguously what it is you are saying.

Going beyond just answering the question

This paragraph should be read with extreme caution! Students often try to go beyond the question set without truly answering the question first. You should not speculate what a better question would have looked like then answer this one (yes we have seen this!) We recommend that you perhaps look at adding a very short section which draws wider conclusions from the material presented. Perhaps implications for how the area of study is developing or latest thinking/debates in the field. This should be extremely short and you must make it clear that you have finished answering the essay question and that this is just an additional piece to demonstrate your in-depth knowledge of the material. Only advanced students should attempt this – and anyway it is really tricky to gain marks by doing this. Perhaps something to try once you are completely confident about your essay writing and probably when you are feeling a bit cocky. Make sure it doesn't make you sound like a smart aleck though!

Read and commented on line by line by someone else

This is again a bit tricky to do as these days very few lecturers outside Oxford and Cambridge have the time to comment in detail on essays before they are submitted. If you want to do this, you will need to find someone who has both the expertise and the time to comment on your work in detail. In other words, someone who is able to say whether or not you have really understood (a) the question set and (b) the material you have gathered – and whether you have really used (b) to fully answer (a). There might be a friendly tutor willing to do this, perhaps your library provides tutors to do this sort of work. One possibility is that you arrange yourself into an informal study group where you provide this service to one another. This is an excellent practice but can be very dangerous if you are all answering the same essay question as you could open yourselves to charges of collusion if the essays end up looking too similar. So do be careful if you decide to try to follow this line.

Reread before submission

This was of course recommended for the basic level. However, experience shows that students frequently skip this step and you can really tell when you read their essays! Don't get too hung up about this stage though because if you read and reread too much you could start undoing the great work you have put into the essay by tinkering with it too much. But, you should reread at least once. You are far better off doing this after a decent break after you have finished writing. In this way you read your work as if for the first time and often mistakes will jump out at you. Probably as often you will read it and be pleased with yourself as it may actually be better than you had thought.

With your essay completely written, we now turn to making sure the referencing is correct.

Chapter 6

How to Reference Correctly

Chapter objectives

Having read this chapter you will:

- know why you need to use references
- understand that the format needs to be followed precisely
- know the difference between the Harvard and Chicago styles
- understand how to place references in your text
- know how the two styles work and how to use them.

Students often come to us and tell us that referencing is one of the most confusing concepts for them when writing essays or reports for university courses. Not only are there various types of referencing styles, but each style also has so many different variations regarding the way you need to reference sources within essays. To address these concerns we have decided to allocate one chapter to the issue of referencing and another to a quiz on referencing so you can test yourself and make sure you really understand how to do this essential component of essay writing. We have found over the years that referencing generates most questions from students and is probably responsible for the most worry. So we hope the following will teach you exactly how to reference – in straightforward terms. Once learned, you will remember it for ever and save yourself untold worry at university.

Let's make it clear from the start; there is no set number of references you should use to get the best marks. The number of references depends on how many you think are necessary to support your arguments. However, one reference per statement is probably enough until you get to a very advanced level or you are trying to make a point very strongly. As a general guideline, however, keep in mind that showing that you have gone beyond the set reading list will almost certainly get you better marks than if you just use the set textbook as a reference for your entire essay. No matter how many references you use, make sure that the references support your argument and make your essay a stronger piece. This will earn you the best marks.

So why bother referencing?

The reason for referencing is actually quite simple. You are acknowledging that the ideas, theories and findings you are using for your essay are someone else's work and not your own. Think of it this way, if you came up with a great idea and then heard someone else talking as if it were theirs, you would be naturally quite insulted. The same applies to you using other people's work. You do not want to be 'stealing' someone else's work. There is another (and perhaps more positive reason) for referencing which is: by citing the work of a scholar in a peer-reviewed journal you are saying two things to the marker:

- 'It's not me saying this but an expert, so it must be true'

- 'Look at me – I've read this paper/chapter/book and I know my stuff'.

So by referencing a theory or finding, you are telling the reader that this is not what you have come up with but you are using another person's work to form an argument and back up your own claims. The latter is one of the most common causes of confusion among students. A lot of times when students are asking about their essays, they ask me why they need to reference general knowledge. What we always tell them is that, although it might well be common knowledge now, it was once found or established by an individual or a group of people. Let us take gravity as an example. Yes, we all are aware that there is something called gravity which will pull objects towards the centre of the earth. So when we drop an apple, the apple will fall towards the ground with a certain speed. The force behind this is gravity. Despite pretty much everyone being aware of it, the individual who first realised this process and defined the concept of gravity was Sir Isaac Newton. You now see that 'general knowledge' in your essay was once identified, defined or found by someone. It is, therefore, necessary that you acknowledge this by using references. Of course there are certain things which it might be difficult to attribute to one particular person or group and it might be difficult for you to identify the source of knowledge. Also be aware that what you think of as being 'common knowledge' may not actually be either common (many people might not know it) or knowledge (other people might disagree with your idea of what is right or accepted). However, it is important that you try to identify who (if anyone) made the same claim as you. Your best way of finding a source is to use an Internet search engine. These usually point you in the right direction so that you do not have to go through a million books trying to find something while you could be working on finishing your essay. BUT, do be very careful about the sources that they point you to – only use credible, academically rigorous sources (see Chapter 4).

Finally, the most important reason for you to reference is plagiarism. Many of you may be familiar with the concept of plagiarism, but let's quickly recap (this is covered in full in Chapter 8 but we introduce the idea here as it is will help you understand what referencing is about). You saw above that it is important to acknowledge others' work. If you fail to do so, claiming that it is your own work, or not making it clear to the reader that your arguments, claims or assumptions are not your intellectual property, you commit plagiarism. Plagiarism is a serious offence, not only at university but also in areas such as journalism. If you are caught plagiarising at university you may risk being expelled or face other disciplinary measures. We will talk about plagiarism, how to avoid it and look at some examples in the next chapter. But let us first look at how to make sure your referencing is up to standard, giving you the extra points needed for a good essay and course mark.

Different types of referencing

There is a rather curious thing about academic life: you are encouraged to question everything you are told but there are also some things which you just have to accept and follow the rules. The essay as a whole is one example of this and references are another. Here's the basic rule:

FOLLOW THE FORMAT ABSOLUTELY – 100 PER CENT

There is no room for you to adopt your own style or to do it more or less right. You must do it *exactly* in the format you are given. There isn't a particular reason for this except perhaps to make your essays easier to understand. Confusingly there are several different formats and, indeed, universities often have their own particular take on what format to use. In the absence of any esoteric reference system at your university, we recommend you follow one of the following formats which we think are the most common. At our university (Aston) we happen to use the Harvard system and this is very common in the journals we publish in.

So we will look at the two most widely used ones for academic essays: the Harvard referencing system, also known as the author–date or the APA (American Psychological Association) system, and the Chicago referencing style. With the Chicago style we will focus on how to reference using footnotes. There is no better or worse style, it is simply up to your course requirements which type of style you should use for your essay. So check with your tutor.

This chapter will be structured along the lines in the following box.

The Harvard referencing style (author–date/ APA system) – in-text references

The idea of this system is for you to write the author's name and the year of publication in brackets after you use their work in the text of the essay. You then include the full details of the work in a list at the end of the essay. For example:

> The physiological and psychological effects of stress can be measured much in the way that physical strain on materials can be measured (Hinkle, 1973).

What this does is to show that it isn't just you making this up, it is the result of scientific work carried out by the much revered and respected Lawrence Hinkle. If readers hadn't read this paper or need to be reminded about it, all they need do is turn to the alphabetical list of references you provide at the end of your essay and they would find the full listing for this paper:

> Hinkle, L.E. (1973) 'The concept of stress in the biological and social sciences', *Science Medicine and Man*, 1: 31–48.

So if they were so inclined the reader could now go to the library, find all the volumes of *Science Medicine and Man*, look along the shelf until they reached 1973 volume 1 and turn to page 31. So much for the concept, now to the practice.

Some general guidelines

It really is very simple to work out the basic format for the in-text element of the reference:

> Text (surname, year) text

Before we start with examples of in-text references, let's start with one of the main confusions regarding referencing. In a lot of first year essays, we come across students who reference not only the author's name and the year but also include the author's first name or initials or the title of the book. Some will even give you the place of publication. In fact all you are allowed to provide in your in-text references is the name and the year of the source.

There is a slight refinement needed when making a direct quote (that is, using the precise words written by someone else), you also need the page number; however, if you have summarised a concept, you should just put the author's surname and year. Just take a look the general guidelines in Table 6.1, which you can use as a template. The particulars which should give you templates to work from are also explained later on in the chapter. So enjoy your journey through the world of referencing. It will all look a lot easier once you have seen how it is done.

Table 6.1 Examples of references

Type of source	In-text	Reference list
General guideline	Text (surname, year)	
Any – one author	… Yukl (2006) … … (Yukl, 2006) …	Yukl, G. (2006). *Leadership in Organizations*, 6th ed. New Jersey: Pearson.
Any – two authors	… Bass and Steidlmeier (1999) … … (Bass & Steidlmeier, 1999) …	Bass, B.M. & Steidlmeier, P. (1999). Ethics, character, and authentic transformational leadership behavior. *Leadership Quarterly, 10*(2), 181–217.
Any – three authors	… Meindl, Ehrlich, and Dukerich (1985) … … (Meindl, Ehrlich, & Dukerich, 1985) …	Meindl, J.R., Ehrlich, S.B., & Dukerich, J.M. (1985). The romance of leadership. *Administrative Science Quarterly, 30*(1), 78–102.
Any – three authors – subsequent use	… Meindl et al. (1985) … … (Meindl et al., 1985) …	
Any – four to six authors	… Remenyi, Williams, Money, and Swartz (2005) … … (Remenyi, Williams, Money, & Swartz, 2005) …	Remenyi, D., Williams, B., Money, A., & Swartz, E. (2005). *Doing Research in Business and Management*. London: Sage Publications.
Any – four to six authors – subsequent use	… Remenyi et al. (2005) … … (Remenyi et al., 2005) …	
Any – more than six authors	… GLOBE (House et al., 2004)	House, R.J., Hanges, P.J., Javidan, M., Dorfman, P.W., Gupta, V., & associates (2004). *Culture, Leadership and Organisations: The GLOBE Study of 62 Societies*. London: Sage Publications.
Edited books	… Britt and Dickinson (2006) …	Britt, T.W., & Dickinson, J.M. (2006). Morale during military operations: a positive psychology approach. In T.W. Britt, C.A. Castro, & A.B. Adler (Eds), *Military Life: The Psychology of Serving in Peace and Combat C* (vol.1: pp. 157–84). Westport, CT:Praeger Security International.
Quotes	… (Yukl, 2006, p. 229) …	Yukl, G. (2006). *Leadership in Organizations*, 6th ed. New Jersey: Pearson.

The following examples apply to almost all possible sources you may come across, including books, articles, newspaper articles, Internet resources. Whenever you can identify the author, the following examples can be used as a template for your own essays.

Referencing one author

Author as part of sentence:

> Yukl (2006) argues that the main ingredients of effective ethical leadership are to walk the talk and create an environment of collaboration minimizing politics and secrecy.

Author in parentheses:

> The main ingredients of effective ethical leadership are to walk the talk and create an environment of collaboration minimizing politics and secrecy (Yukl, 2006).

So you see from the above examples that you can use two different styles of writing. In the first example the author is part of the sentence, while in the second example the author is placed in brackets. The reason is really only a stylistic one. It is up to you to decide whether you think your sentence achieves a better flow by including the author's name as part of the sentence or whether putting it at the end, in parentheses, makes it a smoother read. The choice is yours and with time you will get a feel for what works best and when to use what. There is really no right or wrong here but you might also like to make sure you mix them up so you don't use the same method the whole time.

Referencing two to three authors

We are trying to make this as much a template you can work from as possible and that is why we will now show you the reference techniques for two and three authors. Let us assume you had two authors contributing to an article, a book or a chapter. Obviously now you need to acknowledge both authors. Many students tend to use the et al. option at this point or only reference one of the authors. However, as we have seen before, it is really important to mention both authors. Look at the following examples.

Two authors as part of sentence:

> Indirect negative relationships are characterised by, what Bass and Steidlmeier (1999) named, pseudo-transformational leadership, a form of unethical leadership.

Two authors in brackets:

> Indirect negative relationships are characterised by pseudo-transformational leadership, a form of unethical leadership (Bass & Steidlmeier, 1999).

The important distinction here is the '&' versus the 'and' between the two names. Always make sure that you use '&' when the names are in brackets and use 'and' when the author names are part of the sentence.

How about three authors? Well, it is pretty much the same as above, you simply have to list all three names.

Three authors as part of sentence:

> We can conclude from Meindl, Ehrlich, and Dukerich (1985) that, in order to grasp possible links between unethical leadership and increased performance, it is useful to look at the romance of leadership debate

Three authors in parentheses:

> In order to grasp possible links between unethical leadership and increased performance, it is useful to look at the romance of leadership debate (Meindl, Ehrlich, & Dukerich, 1985).

Now this is where it gets a bit interesting. Some of you may have seen the earlier mentioned et al. – which means, simply, 'and others'. As the first person of an article, book or any other paper is usually considered the main author, we can use his or her name and et al. when using three authors repetitively.

In other words, if you were to use Meindl, Ehrlich, and Dukerich in the above example more than once in your essay, you no longer need to write all their names, but use the first name and et al. You will, therefore, only have to write out all three names the first time you use something they have said. In subsequent instances, all you need to do in this example is to write Meindl et al.

So when you use their names for the first time in your essay write them out as above. When using them for the second, third or any subsequent time, all you do is:

Three authors as part of sentence – subsequent use:

> As Meindl et al. (1985) said, perception of leadership may be influenced by past performance.

Three authors in parentheses – subsequent use:

> Perception of leadership may be influenced by past performance (Meindl et al., 1985).

Referencing four to six authors and over six authors

We have now covered the basics so can easily work from this foundation and build up the numbers of authors. There is not much change, except that the number of authors now increases to four to six authors. Let's look at two examples for four authors:

Four authors as part of sentence:

> Remenyi, Williams, Money and Swartz (2005) state that the phenomenological or constructivist paradigm attempts to understand phenomena in the light of multiple realities.

Four authors in parentheses:

> The phenomenological or constructivist paradigm attempts to understand phenomena in the light of multiple realities (Remenyi, Williams, Money & Swartz, 2005).

Just as for three authors, subsequent use of four to six author names only requires you to write the main/first author and et al. This can be quite useful when considering word counts for essays, because you may be able to save quite a number of words and use them for your arguments.

Four authors as part of sentence – subsequent use:

> Remenyi et al. (2005) also argue that the phenomenological paradigm is a more holistic way of comprehending realities.

Four authors in parentheses – subsequent use:

> The phenomenological paradigm is a more holistic way of comprehending realities (Remenyi et al., 2005).

If you now were to come across an article, book or any other type of source you are using for your essay, there is no need to ever cite more than six authors. So in a case of more than six authors, all you need to do is reference the first six authors.

More than six authors as part of sentence:

> In a six-study design Clary, Snyder, Ridge, Copeland, Stukas, Haugen et al. (1998) set out to investigate the motivational mechanisms underlying volunteering.

More than six authors in parentheses:

> The motivational mechanisms underlying volunteering were explored in a six-study design (Clary, Snyder, Ridge, Copeland, Stukas, Haugen et al., 1998).

More than six authors as part of sentence – subsequent use:

Clary et al. (1998) identified several of the motivational mechanisms contributing to someone's willingness to volunteer.

More than six authors in parentheses – subsequent use:

Several of the motivational mechanisms contributing to someone's willingness to volunteer were identified (Clary et al., 1998).

Referencing edited books

There will be times when you read a book containing various chapters written by different authors. This type of book is called an edited book and is one in which the editor or editors have invited other people to contribute to the book by writing chapters on their area of expertise. Usually textbooks tend to be non-edited books – that is, books that are written by the people you find on the cover. However, a lot of other books are edited versions for which we need to use a slightly different approach regarding referencing. Let us look at an example:

Britt and Dickinson (2006) regard morale as a type of motivation variable.

Now Britt and Dickinson wrote a chapter in a book edited by Britt, Castro and Adler published in 2006. As it is Britt and Dickinson you are referencing, all you need to do in your text is to cite Britt and Dickinson's name and the year the edited book was published, 2006.

Referencing conference papers

When referencing conference papers, all you need to do is to proceed as outlined in our examples above. You should find the name of the person who presented the paper at a conference on top of the first page, just as on a journal article.

Referencing resources with no particular author

Sometimes when you come across online resources, papers published by an agency such as a government body or another type of organisation (e.g., a consultancy), newspaper articles or press releases, you may not be able to identify a particular person responsible for the publication. You will then have to use the organisation's name as the author's name. If you are able to pinpoint a particular author, then just follow the guidelines described above. For the cases where you are unable to do so, let us look at some examples.

An organisation (e.g., public or private):

> As CBI (2000) estimates suggest, 196 million days were lost in 1998 due to sickness.

A newspaper article:

> *The Economic Newsscout* (1997) argues for an increase in public spending.

A press release or annual report:

> BMW (2006) announces an increase in sales.

A dictionary or encyclopaedia:

> *The Oxford English Dictionary* (1989, p. 287) defines need as a 'necessity arising from the facts and circumstances of the case.'

Referencing lecture notes

This is a particular issue. A lot of lecturers will tell you not to use their own lecture as a reference. To be on the safe side, check with your lecturer. We generally advise our students to reference the original source; however, at times they might not be able to find an original source so we let them off and allow them to use our lecture notes as a reference.

Referencing your lecture notes is pretty much the same as in the examples you have seen so far. All you need to do is use your lecturer's surname and the year.

Quotations

> The most incomprehensible thing about the world is that it is at all comprehensible. (Albert Einstein)

We have looked at all the different formats of references depending on the number of authors and where to place the reference in your sentence. Let us now turn to something that a lot of students use in their first academic essays: quotations. It is important to mention upfront that as long as you are able to put something into your own words, you should do so. In other words, try to minimise the use of quotations as much as possible. It never looks good if your entire essay is full of quotations because it only shows the examiner that you are able to use copy and paste, but not that you actually understand what is said. The easiest way of avoiding quotations and making use of your own writing and thinking skills is by reading something first and then imagining you are telling someone in your own words what you have just read (or if you have a very patient housemate, friend or partner you can actually 'abuse' their good nature). After reading something, give it about 30 or so seconds and your memory is unlikely to retrieve the exact wording but rather will recall the quintessence wrapped in your own words. Only use quotations when it is absolutely unavoidable, such as in the case of many definitions. Your essay is your work and, therefore, should be comprised of your own words. Minimising the use of quotations and maximising your own input will also allow you to form a more coherent and structured piece. It will also help you to understand theories, ideas and findings better (which might be very useful if you have an exam on the topic at a later point). Just as Einstein said, when something appears difficult to comprehend, put it into your own words and it becomes comprehensible. Sometimes, however, it is difficult to avoid quotations such as in the case of some precise definition or because you want to use someone's quote to base an argument on or use it to strengthen what you are trying to say.

Quotations (the word limit)   When using quotations, you may have to use two different ways of including them in your essay. Depending on the length of the quote you are using, you have to adapt the way it is incorporated. Let us look at the two different ways of using quotations depending on their length.

Up to three lines   Up to three lines, you can simply incorporate the quote as part of your sentence. Just take a look at the following example:

> Ability is 'the extent to which unit members understand their individual job responsibilities, know what to do, and have the skills to do it' (Yukl, 2006, p. 229).

More than three lines   If your quote contains more than three lines, include the quote not as part of a sentence, but allocate a separate indented paragraph to it as in the following example:

> An interesting point made by Wicks and Freeman (1998) with regard to the importance of epistemology in organisation studies:
>
> > Epistemology helps shape whether – and how – ethics (i.e., advancing human purposes) is part of research. Avoiding discussion of ethics and trying to remain agnostic on the subject does not allow positivist researchers to make organization studies value-free (Wicks & Freeman, 1998, p. 124).
>
> However, as mentioned above ...

Same author – multiple works

Sometimes you will find that one person has published multiple works in one year. If you come across such a case, you will need to make use of letters after the year:

Training leaders in transformational leadership can have very positive effects for the individual (Bass, 1990a).

Bass (1990b) argues that transformational leadership has a positive effect on performance.

Referencing a secondary source

First, let us be clear what primary and secondary sources are:

- *Primary source*: A book, article, paper, or any other source you actually read yourself. This does not mean reading the entire book, but at least the section you are using for your essay.

- *Secondary source*: A book, article, paper or any other source that is referenced in a document you are reading. The only source you have read is, therefore, the latter document, not the actual source.

Referencing a secondary source is one of the most confusing issues for a lot of students. Secondary referencing means nothing more than reading someone's work referenced in an article, book or any other primary source. You have, therefore, not read the actual work – such as an article reporting findings – you are referencing. What you have read is someone else's work, such as a textbook, reporting that Mr X has found that apples are round.

Confused? Don't be, let's have a look at a couple of examples.

Imagine you read in your textbook that one day a man named Vroom came up with something called the expectancy theory of motivation. Now, the text in your textbook is likely to read something like:

Vroom (1964) argued that motivation is partly dependent on the extent a person expects the outcome to be favorable.

Particularly at the beginning of your academic career, you are unlikely to have actually read Vroom. Even if you have only read the textbook, you may still use Vroom as a reference in your essay. The only difference is the way in which you tell readers where they can find Vroom's theory in your textbook. In order to make it easier for the reader to find the source you are using and to get better marks in your essay, use the following way of referencing.

Secondary source as part of sentence:

Vroom (1964, cited in Fincham & Rhodes, 2005, p. 208) argues that a person's motivation depends on the extent the outcome is expected to be favourable.

Secondary source in parentheses:

> A person's motivation depends on the extent the outcome is expected to be favourable (Vroom, 1964, cited in Fincham & Rhodes, 2005, p. 208) .

But what should you do if you are using a secondary quote you found in your textbook or an article? Just the same as above.

A secondary source quote:

> Altruism is behaviour that is 'directly and intentionally aimed at helping a specific person in face-to-face situations' (Smith, Organ, & Near, 1983, cited in McAllister, 1995, p. 29).

The Harvard referencing style – the reference list

Now you have referenced all the sources you have used within your essay. That is it, right? Unfortunately, now you have to make sure to tell the reader the exact location where each particular finding, theory or argument can be found. Let me tell you upfront that one of the best things to do while writing your essay is to keep track of which references you are using. Otherwise you will be sitting there for some time trying to find and note down all the references you have used. Make it easier for yourself and just keep a separate document listing all the references you are using. Don't start checking if all your references are there when you start proofreading. At this point you should already have the entire list. This gives you the necessary distance from your own work needed to 'objectively' check whether or not everything is there.

One last word before we move on. Make sure that all your primary references, the ones you have actually read, are listed in *alphabetical order* in the reference list. After all, even though you get to learn interesting aspects of life when writing essays (believe me, you really do, even when only realised in retrospect), it is also about good marks. And the best marks are dependent on whether your work is complete or not. It will also help you to find a reference quickly again when you have to write something on a similar subject and want to reuse a particular source.

Before we look at the specifics, here are some general guidelines on citing references in reference lists.

Some general guidelines

Before we look at the specifics, let us take a look at the general outline of a reference in your reference list by type of resource.

Annual report

Company name. (Year). *Title of report*. Place of publication.

Article

Surname, initials. (Year). Title. *Journal, edition* (volume), pages.

Book

Surname, initials. (Year). *Title*. Place of publication: Publisher.

Edited book

Surname, initials. (Year). Title of chapter. In initials surname (ed.), *Title of Book* (pp.). Place of publication: publisher.

Conference paper

Surname, initials. (Year). Title. *Title*. Paper presented at conference name, place of conference. Retrieved month, day, year, from database.

Newspaper/magazine article – author

Surname, initials. (Year, month day). Title of article. *Publication name*, page.

Newspaper/magazine article – no author

Title. (Year, month day). *Publication name*, page.

Online

Surname, initials. (Year). *Title*. Publisher. Retrieved month, day, year, from http://www.WXYZ.net

Press release

Company name (year, month day). *Title of release*, [type of release].

Using the earlier examples, let us now look how they look when written as part of the reference list.

Referencing one author

Conger, J.A. (1998). Qualitative research as the cornerstone methodology for understanding leadership. *Leadership Quarterly, 9*, 107–121.

Referencing two authors

Bass, B.M. & Steidlmeier, P. (1999). Ethics, character, and authentic transformational leadership behavior. *Leadership Quarterly, 10*(2), 181–217.

Referencing three authors

Meindl, J.R., Ehrlich, S.B., & Dukerich, J.M. (1985). The romance of leadership. *Administrative Science Quarterly, 30*(1), 78–102.

Referencing four to six authors

Remenyi, D., Williams, B., Money, A., & Swartz, E. (2005). *Doing Research in Business and Management.* London: Sage Publications.

Referencing more than six authors

Just as with the in-text reference, all you need to do here is list the first six authors:

Clary, E.G., Snyder, M., Ridge, R.D., Copeland, J., Stukas, A.A., Haugen, J. et al. (1998). Understanding and assessing the motivations of volunteers: a functional approach. *Journal of Personality and Social Psychology, 74*(6), 1516–1530.

Referencing books

Yukl, G. (2006). *Leadership in Organizations*, 6th ed. New Jersey: Pearson.

Referencing a chapter in an edited book

Britt, T.W. & Dickinson, J.M. (2006). Morale during military operations: a positive psychology approach. In T.W. Britt, C.A. Castro, & A.B. Adler (Eds.), *Military Life: The Psychology of Serving in Peace and Combat* (vol.1: pp. 157–184). Westport, CT: Praeger Security International.

Referencing online resources

Craig, J. (2006, June 17). The cons of being a pro. The *Guardian*. Retrieved June 26, 2006, from http://money.guardian.co.uk/print/0,,329506605-117763,00.html.

Referencing conference papers

Britt, T.W. & Bliese, P. (1998). *Leadership, perceptions of work, and the stress-buffering effects of job engagement.* Colloquium presented at the Center for Creative Leadership as winner of the Walter F. Ulmer Applied Research Award.

Referencing quotations

There is nothing you need to do differently when listing a quote source in your reference list. Let's take our earlier quote example and see what it would look like in a reference list:

Wicks, A.C. & Freeman, R.E. (1998). Organisation studies and the new pragmatism: positivism, anti-positivism, and the search for ethics. *Organization Science, 9*(2), 123–140.

So you see, there is no need to indicate the actual page. You have already done so in your text and don't need to do it again here.

Annual report

BMW (2006). *Annual report 2006*. Munich: BMW AG.

Press release

Masterflex AG (2007, December 18). *Masterflex AG continues to enjoy success*, [Ad hoc]. Gelsenkirchen.

Newspaper/magazine article – author

Budworth, D. (2008, January 27). How to ride the market rollercoaster. *The Sunday Times*, 1.

Newspaper/magazine article – no author

Demographic change requires increase in public spending. (1997, May 23). *The Economic Newsscout*, 4.

An organisation (e.g., public or private)

CBI (2000). *Focus on absence: absence and labour turnover survey 2000*. UK: Confederation of British Industry.

Encyclopaedia or dictionary

The Oxford English Dictionary. (2nd ed., Vol. X). (1989). Oxford: University Press.

Referencing the same author more than once within the same year

When you use two papers by the same author in the same year, all you need to do is add a letter after the year to show the reader which is which reference, just as you have done in the text. Now simply add the full reference for both sources.

Bass (1990a). *Bass and Stogdill's Handbook of Leadership: Theory, Research & Managerial Applications.* New York: The Free Press.

Bass (1990b). From transactional to transformational leadership: Learning to share the vision. *Organizational Dynamics, 18*(3), 19–31.

Referencing a secondary source

As mentioned earlier, this tends to be quite confusing when you first come to university. A lot of students put a lot more work into this than is actually necessary. The good news is that all you need to do is list the primary source here. So if you were to use your textbook as your main source for your essay (which is likely to be the case for your first essay), then all you need to list here in the reference list is your textbook. Let's take a look at our earlier example: there is no need to show the reference for Vroom here, all you need to do is to give the textbook reference:

Fincham, R. & Rhodes, P. (2005). *Principles of Organisational Behaviour* (4th ed). Oxford: Oxford University Press.

Now we have looked at the different main categories of referencing. You might come across some sources that are not shown here. Usually you will find that they are referenced similarly to the ones we have just discussed. But to make sure always check with your library or consult the Internet with its many valuable sources.

The Chicago referencing style – footnotes

This section of the reference chapter will introduce and explain how to use footnotes for reference purposes, followed by a final section on the reference list according to the Chicago style. This style is often used in economics courses at business schools, but you will also find it in many other areas of academic life and outside. We will use the earlier examples to show you the difference between what the two styles will look like when you use them in your essay or report. Let us now look at the below text to see how it is done. The borders of the box represent a page of your essay.

The main ingredients of effective ethical leadership are to walk the talk and create an environment of collaboration minimizing politics and secrecy.[1]

Yet, indirect negative relationships are characterized by pseudo-transformational leadership, a form of unethical leadership.[2]

In order to grasp possible links between unethical leadership and increased performance, it is useful to look at the romance of leadership debate.[3]

The phenomenological or constructivist paradigm attempts to understand phenomena in the light of multiple realities.[4]

The term pro has lost part of its true meaning and strength.[5]

The motivational mechanisms underlying volunteering were explored in a six-study design.[6]

Interestingly, morale has been regarded as a type of motivation variable.[7]

As estimates suggest, 196 million days were lost in 1998 due to sickness.[8]

Therefore, *The Economic Newsscout* argues for an increase in public spending.[9]

BMW, on the other hand, announces an increase in sales.[10]

The Oxford English Dictionary defines need as 'a necessity arising from the facts and circumstances of the case'.[11]

Ability is 'the extent to which unit members understand their individual job responsibilities, know what to do, and have the skills to do it.'[12]

Training leaders in transformational leadership can have very positive effects for the individual.[13]

Transformational leadership has been suggested to have a positive effect on performance.[14]

Fincham and Rhodes state that Vroom argued that motivation is partly dependent on the extent a person expects the outcome to be favourable.[15]

[1] Gary Yukl, *Leadership in Organizations*, 6th ed. (New Jersey: Pearson, 2006), 53.

[2] Bernard Bass and Paul Steidlmeier, 'Ethics, character, and authentic transformational leadership behavior,' *Organisational Dynamics* 18, no.3 (1990): 45.

[3] James R. Sanford, B. Meindl, Ehrlich and Janet M. Dukerich, 'The romance of leadership', *Administrative Science Quarterly* 30, no.1 (1985): 56.

[4] Dan Remenyi, Brian williams, Arthur Money and Ethne Swartz, *Doing Research in Business and Management* (London: Sage Publications, 2005): 23.

[5] John Craig, 'The cons of being a pro', The *Guardian*, June 17, 2006. http://money.guardian.co.uk/print/0,329506605–117763,00. html.

[6] Gil E. Clary et al., 'Understanding and assessing the motivations of volunteers: a functional approach', *Journal of Personality and Social Psychology* 74, no.6 (1998): 56.

[7] Thomas W. Britt and Paul Dickinson, 'Morale during military operations: a positive psychology approach', in *Military Life: The Psychology of Serving in Peace and Combat*, ed. T.W. Britt, C.A. Castro and Amy B. Adler (Westport, CT: Praeger Security International, 2006): 165.

[8] CBI. *Focus on absence: Absence and labour turnover survey* 2000, 7.

[9] *The Economic Newsscout*, 'Demographic change requires increase in public spending', May 23, 1997: 4.

[10] BMW, *Annual report* 2006, 45.

[11] *The Oxford English Dictionary*, 2nd, vol X, 287.

[12] Yukl, *Leadership in Organizations*, 229.

[13] Bernard Bass, *Bass and Stogdill's Handbook of Leadership: Theory, Research & Managerial Applications*, (New York: The Free Press, 1990): 387.

[14] Bernard Bass, 'From transactional to transformational leadership: Learning to share the vision', *Organizational Dynamics*, 18, no.3 (1990): 156.

[15] Robin Fincham and Peter Rhodes, *Principles of Organizational Behaviour*, (Oxford: Oxford University Press, 2005): 356.

[16] Yukl, 327.

Subsequent use of the same source

Before we move on to the reference list according to the Chicago referencing style, just a word of warning: despite the above referencing looking like quite some work, subsequent use of the same sources becomes easier and requires less effort.

All you have to do when using a source such as Yukl again is to write the author's name and the page you have got the theory, idea, argument or any other information from. It would then look like this on the bottom of your page:

The Chicago referencing style – reference list

Just as with the Harvard referencing style, you will then need to create a bibliography in an alphabetical order. The difference with the Chicago style is the way the reference list is written.

References

Bass, Bernard. *Bass and Stogdill's Handbook of Leadership: Theory, Research & Managerial Applications*. New York: The Free Press, 1990.

Bass, Bernard. 'From transactional to transformational leadership: Learning to share the vision.' *Organizational Dynamics*, 18, no.3 (1990): 19–31.

Bass, Bernard M. & Steidlmeier, Paul. 'Ethics, character, and authentic transformational leadership behavior.' *Leadership Quarterly* 10, no.2 (1999): 181–217.

BMW. *Annual report 2006*. Munich: BMW AG, 2006.

Britt, Thomas W. & Bliese, Paul. *Leadership, perceptions of work, and the stress-buffering effects of job engagement*. Colloquium presented at the Center for Creative Leadership as winner of the Walter F. Ulmer Applied Research Award, 1998.

Britt, Thomas.W. & Dickinson, James M. 'Morale during military operations: a positive psychology approach.' In *Military Life: The Psychology of Serving in Peace and Combat*. Vol 1, edited by Thomas.W. Britt, Carl A. Castro, and Amy B. Adler, 157–184. Westport, CT: Praeger Security International, 2006.

Clary, Gil E., Snyder, Mark, Ridge, Robert D., Copeland, John, Stukas, Arthur A., Haugen, Julie & Miene, Peter. 'Understanding and assessing the motivations of volunteers: Functional approach.' *Journal of Personality and Social Psychology* 74, no.6 (1998): 1516–1530.

Craig, John. 'The cons of being a pro.' The *Guardian*, June 17, 2006. http://money.guardian.co.uk/print/0,,329506605-117763,00.html.

Demographic change requires increase in public spending. *The Economic Newsscout*, 1997, May 23: 4.

Fincham, Robin & Rhodes, Peter. *Principles of Organisational Behaviour,* 4th ed. Oxford: Oxford University Press, 2005.

Masterflex AG. *Masterflex AG continues to enjoy success*, [Ad hoc]. Gelsenkirchen; 2007, December 18.

Meindl, James R., Ehrlich, Sanford B., & Dukerich, Janet M. 'The romance of leadership.' *Administrative Science Quarterly* 30, no.1 (1985): 78–102.

[No note for *The Oxford English Dictionary* reference. Usually well-known references are cited as a footnote and not in the bibliography.]

Remenyi, Dan, Williams, Brian, Money, Arthur & Swartz, Ethne. *Doing Research in Business and Management*. London: Sage Publications, 2005.

Yukl, Gary. *Leadership in Organizations*, 6th ed. New Jersey: Pearson, 2006.

You have now seen how to write references in two different ways, according to two distinct styles: Harvard and Chicago. The way you should write them depends on your course requirements so always check with your school and tutor. The next chapter will show you why knowing how to reference correctly is so important when writing your essay.

Chapter 7

The Great Big Referencing Quiz

Chapter objectives

Having read this chapter, you will:

- have practised how to format references in the text
- have practised how to format a list of references at the end of the essay.

The most important thing when it comes to referencing is actually to understand which information you have to use for your own reference.

The reference quiz (part one)

The first part of the reference quiz will give you the opportunity to practice your knowledge of how to reference a journal article, a book and an online reference. You will see an example of each of these source types and will have to show:

- how you would write the in-text reference; and

- how you would write the reference in the reference list.

First you will do this for each individual example and finally put together a reference list with the sources you are given below.

To answer Questions 1 and 2 on p. 75 refer to the journal article in Figure 7.1.

Trust in Organizational Superiors: Systemic and Collective Considerations

Boas Shamir, Yael Lapidot

Abstract

Boas Shamir
Hebrew University
of Jerusalem,
Israel

Yael Lapidot
College of
Management, Tel
Aviv, Israel

The social-psychological literature on trust in organizational superiors implies that it is an interpersonal phenomenon, based on the superior's behaviours and on subordinates' perceptions of the superior's behaviours and qualities. The sociological literature, in contrast, implies that trust in a superior is a property of the system in which the superior–subordinate relationship is embedded. In this article, we suggest that trust is both an interpersonal and a collective phenomenon and focus on the linkages between three levels of trust: the system level, the group level, and the individual level. We use a longitudinal quantitative analysis of cadets' trust in their team commanders and a qualitative analysis of critical incidents of trust building and erosion to develop and support three propositions. First, trust in a superior reflects subordinates' trust in the system that the superior represents. Second, subordinates employ criteria derived from systemic properties such as collective identities and values to evaluate the trustworthiness of their superior. Third, team processes play a major role in the social construction of trust in a superior and in translating systemic considerations into criteria for evaluating superiors' trustworthiness.

Keywords: trust, leaders, teams, values, identity

Much has been written in recent years about trust in organizational authorities. This attention stems from a general belief that recent trends in the organizational field, such as higher rates of environmental and technological change, greater needs for flexibility and cooperation, increased reliance on teams and teamwork, and changes in employment relationships and career patterns, increase the importance of trust in organizations (Mayer et al. 1995; Rousseau et al. 1998).

For instance, Brockner et al. (1997: 558) have recently written, 'As organizations have become flatter and more team-based, organizational authorities' surveillance of their subordinates has given way to less dictatorial modes of interpersonal influence. Perhaps now more than ever, managers' effectiveness depends on their ability to gain the trust of their subordinates.' Summarizing research in this area, Brockner et al. (1997) suggest that trust in organizational authorities increases support for such authorities, higher commitment to the authorities, and willingness to behave in ways that help to further the goals of the organization. Other authors have indicated that trust in authorities may influence members' voluntary acceptance of the

Organization
Studies
24(3): 463–491
Copyright © 2003
SAGE Publications
(London,
Thousand Oaks,
CA & New Delhi)

www.sagepublications.com   0170-8406[200303]24:3;463–491;032912

Figure 7.1   Journal article

Figure 7.1   *(Continued)*

authorities' decisions (Tyler and Degoy 1996), as well as members' voluntary behaviours on behalf of the organization, and organizational citizenship behaviours (Organ 1990; Podsakoff et al. 1990; Konovsky and Pugh 1994).

From a related perspective, many writers on leadership view trust as an essential component of leadership (for example, Bennis and Nanus 1985; Locke et al. 1991; Zand 1972). Some even regard it as a defining component. For instance, Solomon (1996: 80) asserts that 'leadership is an emotional relationship of trust', and Conger and Kanungo (1998: 46) state that 'leading implies fostering changes in followers through the building of trust and credibility'. Followers' trust in the leader occupies a central role in several theories of leadership, either explicitly or implicitly. For instance, the Leader-Member-Exchange theory (Graen and Uhl-Bien 1995) focuses on the quality of the dyadic relationships between the leader and group members, and includes trust as a major component of this relationship. In a similar vein, theories of charismatic leadership by House (1977) and Conger and Kanungo (1998) include a follower's trust in the leader as an essential component of the charismatic relationship.

Several studies examined the antecedents of subordinates' trust in their managers or leaders. Butler (1991) examined the relationship between 'conditions of trust', which include several characteristics of managers' behaviour, such as consistency and honesty, and the overall trust of subordinates in their superiors. Podsakoff et al. (1990) found that subordinates' trust in their managers mediated the relationship between managers' transformational leadership behaviours and subordinates' organizational citizenship behaviours. Conger and Kanungo (1998) have shown that charismatic leader behaviours increase reverence for the leader, which in turn increases trust in the leader. Mayer and his colleagues (Mayer and Davis 1999; Mayer and Gavin 1998) have carried out a number of studies that, in general, support the theoretical propositions put forward by Mayer et al. (1995) in an earlier theoretical paper, namely, that subordinates' trust in their leader depends on the leader's perceived levels of ability, benevolence and integrity.

A common feature shared by these social-psychological theories and studies is that they conceive of trust only as a psychological state at the individual level. In a recent review of the literature, Kramer (1999: 571) notes differences among various theories, but states that 'Despite divergence in such particulars, most trust theories agree that, whatever else its essential features, trust is fundamentally a psychological state.' Trust has been viewed by these theories primarily as an interpersonal phenomenon. Trust building and erosion have been attributed to cognitive and affective processes that occur at the individual level, stemming from the characteristics and behaviours of the trustee.

Systemic Trust

In contrast with the above-mentioned social-psychological literature, the sociological literature on trust emphasizes the systemic level of trust. Writers

(Continued)

Figure 7.1   *(Continued)*

from this perspective (for example, Simmel 1950; Parsons 1951; Luhman 1979; Fukuyama 1995; for a recent review, see Lane 1998) view trust as a quality of social systems that enables the maintenance of social order within the system. Systemic trust is impersonal in two senses. First, it is trust in systems or institutions rather than in specific individuals, and, second, unlike interpersonal trust, it is often not based on the personal experience of the trustor.

However, as several writers have noted, trust in organizations often combines both systemic and interpersonal considerations. For instance, Grey and Garsten (2001) have recently noted that the systemic and interpersonal level of trust are interrelated and affect each other. Following, they argue that a full understanding of systemic (organizational) trust is not possible without reference to the individuals who are members of the system, and a full understanding of personal trust is not possible without understanding the systemic context in which such personal trust (or distrust) develops. In a similar vein, Zaheer et al. (1998) have noted that in organizations, trust can exist at both the systemic and the interpersonal level. They further noted the importance of studying the influence process between these levels, namely, how trust translates from the individual level to the organizational level and from the organizational level to the individual level, and the lack of empirical studies that address this issue.

An important arena in which the interplay between systemic and interpersonal considerations can be studied is trust in formal organizational leaders. Formal leaders stand at the intersection between systemic and interpersonal considerations. Trust in formal leaders is likely to be affected by both systemic considerations, because such leaders represent the organization or the system in the eyes of their subordinates, and interpersonal considerations arising from the interactions between leader and subordinates. Furthermore, the two bases of trust are likely to affect each other. Systemic trust might affect trust in particular leaders, and trust in particular leaders might influence systemic trust. These issues have been ignored in the social-psychological studies of trust in leaders and managers reviewed above.

Therefore, the first purpose of the present study was to contribute to understanding of the relationships between systemic and interpersonal trust and to extend the study of trust in organizational leaders by adding systemic considerations to the interpersonal considerations emphasized by extant theories and studies in this field.

The Role of the Group in the Social Construction of Trust

The second purpose of the study was to explore the role that groups play in the formation of trust and distrust in formal leaders and in translating systemic trust to the interpersonal level. It is implicitly assumed in social-psychological theories and studies of trust in organizational superiors that each subordinate independently forms his or her opinion of the superior as trustworthy or not and reacts accordingly. However, in most organizational situations,

Question 1 How would you reference the journal article in the text?

a) Trust in leadership is becoming an increasingly important factor in organizational effectiveness, which is partly due to flatter organizational designs (_____).

b) 'Formal leaders stand at the intersection between systemic and interpersonal considerations' (_____).

c) _____ argue that leaders are the representatives of the organization.

Question 2 How would you reference the journal article in your reference list?

_____

_____

To answer Questions 3 and 4 on p. 80 refer to the book sample in Figure 7.2.

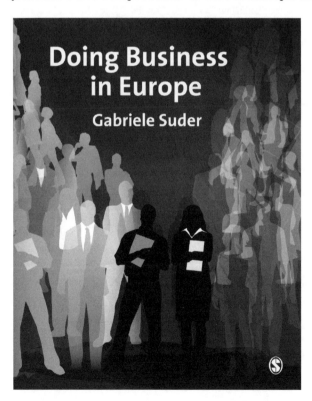

Figure 7.2   Book source

Figure 7.2   *(Continued)*

First published 2008

SAGE Publications Ltd
1 Oliver's Yard
55 City Road
London EC1Y 1SP

SAGE Publications Inc.
2455 Teller Road
Thousand Oaks, California 91320

SAGE Publications India Pvt Ltd
B 1/I 1 Mohan Cooperative Industrial Area
Mathura Road, New Delhi 110 044

SAGE Publications Asia-Pacific Pte Ltd
33 Pekin Street #02-01
Far East Square
Singapore 048763

Library of Congress Control Number: 2006939053

British Library Cataloguing in Publication data

(Continued)

Figure 7.2   *(Continued)*

Introduction: The New European Business Environment

1.1 Centrepiece: The idea of creating a 'unified Europe'

The idea of creating a 'unified Europe' to maintain peace and to create a common European culture has resurfaced repeatedly over European history, although the ideal of a united Europe has its origins in classical philosophical thinking. In the fourteenth century, for example, Pierre Dubois[1] proposed a European confederation that was to be governed by a European council, while in the nineteenth century, Victor Hugo[2] envisaged a political, federal Europe, uniting nations and unifying people. In a speech to the French National Assembly on 1 March 1871 he said:

> Plus de frontières! Le Rhin à tous! Soyons la même République, soyons les États-Unis d'Europe, soyons la fédération continentale, soyons la liberté européenne, soyons la paix universelle!*

Through industrialization and the evolution of trade across frontiers over centuries, nations came to expand their knowledge of different economic systems and trade mechanisms. The end of the feudal system, the mercantilist era from *c.*1600 to *c.*1800, and colonialism shaped societies and their economic and social functioning. The term 'mercantilism' originates from the Latin word *mercari*, meaning 'to run a trade', and from *merx*, meaning 'commodity'. It sets the scene for economic and political interest in internationalization. Mercantilism ideologically underpinned cross-border trade long enough to leave its mark driving exports rather than imports, in so far as a country needed a positive balance of trade to gain more precious metals (gold and silver), and determining that governments introduced tariffs that would inhibit other countries from gaining an economic advantage. The political economist Adam Smith, who is generally considered the father of economics, popularized the term in *The Wealth of Nations* (1776) where he analyzed the exchange mechanisms that drive economies – and indeed, every economic system embraces some exchange activity.

The appeal of harmonious trade for economic growth and welfare developed increasingly from the mid-eighteenth century onwards: more than the dream of peace and stability

---

* 'No more borders! The Rhine to all! Let's be the same Republic, the United States of Europe, let's be the continental federation, let's be the European freedom, let's be the Universal peace!'

(Continued)

Figure 7.2   *(Continued)*

across peoples and nations, the idea of welfare through profitable economic relations was easier to share among all peoples. Adam Smith's book set the foundations for a classical trade theory that evolved strongly on European grounds, and that was complemented in later years by the mainly Anglo-Saxon school of international business research, which analyzed transactions and investments of corporations across borders. It is important at this stage to recognize that the convergence of Europe stems from a basis of economic and philosophical history, and that during the twentieth century this convergence led to pressure on states that had seen their power and sovereignty erode to the benefit of regionalism and globalization. International trade relations thus became key to the fulfilment of the European idea and ideal.

In Europe, economic and political integration have been driven by one predominant fundamental objective: 'Keeping peace among nations'. Interaction between people and their economies has indeed maintained peace for longer than in any other region of the world. Certain European countries have joined together to create a unique organization for this purpose: the European Union (EU). An organization of states, not a confederation, nor an organization of the types generally known in international relations, but rather the most advanced form of economic integration worldwide that is flirting closely with the temptations of political union. As such, the Member States have created a single market that marries competitiveness with certain social ideals (welfare, human rights, equality and many others). The European market place is both the driver and the stimulus of Europe, as it has shaped and is being shaped by the European ideal. It represents the largest economy in the world, the largest trading partner and the largest donor of development assistance.

This market offers opportunities to those corporations that recognize the pros and cons of convergence, and that make the most out of the diversity of cultures, languages, business practices and management styles. At the same time, the challenge for the European institutions is to maintain European developments close to its citizens and to balance a productive economy with social welfare.

The objective of this book is to prepare future managers to face up to the resulting challenges and opportunities for doing business in Europe – a Europe enlarged and deepened through continuous integration. Whether you will be working in a local, a European or an international company, you will be confronted with the issues dealt with in this book. Globalization and Europeanization expose any company operating in or dealing with Europe to those challenges of diversity.

In this introductory chapter, we take a brief look at attitudes among citizens and at some European foundations and symbols, and then introduce some terms and concepts that have a bearing on discussions later in the book.

1.2 Europe: For European citizens and abroad

The European idea and ideal are centred on the citizen and her/his welfare. It is driven by economics and politics, in symbiosis with European competitiveness and its role in the world.

(Continued)

Figure 7.2   *(Continued)*

Box 1   The European Union

The EU, originally known as the European Economic Community (EEC) prior to 1993, is a highly advanced form of economic integration. It is a market grouping of more than 27 countries that promotes the economic wealth of its members not only through barrier-free trade, but also through many other coordinated activities such as a common competition policy, internal and external trade policy, research and development policy, industrial and social policy, and so on. The creation of a central European bank and the adoption of a common currency, the euro, significantly contribute to its singular nature in the world. The EU operates as one economic unit in international trade negotiations.

The EU therefore regularly studies the attitudes of its citizens.[3] Among the statistics that are found in these surveys, it is noteworthy that more than 9 in 10 EU citizens feel that it is extremely or very important to help others and to value people for who they are, while more than 8 in 10 believe that it is important to be involved in creating a better society. These societal values are strong in each Member State.

At the same time, EU citizens seem to appreciate specific identity and traditionalism. Nearly 7 in 10 want to live in a world in which people live by traditional values. We are a long way from a standardization or homogeneity of the peoples of Europe; for business, this is where challenges of values and diversity unfold.

Box 2   EU Member States: Who are they?

In 2007, the EU comprised the following 27 Member States: Austria, Belgium, Bulgaria, Cyprus, Czech Republic, Denmark, Estonia, Germany, Greece, Finland, France, Hungary, Ireland, Italy, Latvia, Lithuania, Luxembourg, Malta, Poland, Portugal, Romania, Slovakia, Slovenia, Spain, Sweden, The Netherlands, United Kingdom (UK).

Is there a European identity among citizens? Again, EU statistics, as well as student surveys conducted by the author at several business schools, illustrate that the majority of EU citizens feel to some extent 'European', in particular those who travel or work across frontiers, while they preserve a strong feeling of adherence to particular roots and culture. Eurostat (the Statistical Office of the European Communities) notes that this feeling of adherence differs greatly among countries: people in Luxembourg are most likely to feel themselves to be European only. This is much higher than in any of the other countries and

Question 3 How would you reference the book source in the text?

a) Peace among nations is the driving force for economic and political integration (_____).

b) 'The end of the feudal system, the mercantilist era from c.1600 to c.1800, and colonialism shaped societies and their economic and social functioning' (_____).

c) _____ states that the open European market offers a great diversity of opportunities.

Question 4 How would you reference the book in your reference list?

_____

_____

To answer Questions 5 and 6 below, refer to the online reference in Figure 7.3.

Question 5 How would you reference this corporate news? (Hint: the article was accessed 22 June 2008.)

a) BMW sales went up from last year (_____).

b) 'BMW brand grows by 2.0%', (_____).

c) _____ reports that Rolls-Royce is also experiencing positive effects.

Question 6 How would you reference the corporate source in your reference list?

_____

_____

To answer Question 7 refer to the three sources used in Question 1 to 6.

Question 7 Put together a reference list using all the above references

Figure 7.3   Corporate news online

Solutions to the reference quiz (part one)

Question 1

a) (Shamir & Lapidot, 2003)

b) (Shamir & Lapidot, 2003, p. 465)

c) Shamir and Lapidot (2003)

Question 2

Shamir, B. & Lapidot, Y. (2003). Trust in organizational superiors: systemic and collective considerations. *Organization Studies, 24*(3), 463–491.

Question 3

a) (Suder, 2008)

b) (Suder, 2008, p. 1)

c) Suder (2008)

Question 4

Suder, G. (2008). *Doing business in Europe.* London: Sage.

Question 5

a) (BMW, 2008)

b) (BMW, 2008)

c) BMW (2008)

Question 6

BMW (2008). *Corporate News.* Retrieved 22 June 2008, from http://www.bmwgroup.com/e/0_0_www_bmwgroup_com/investor_relations/corporate_news/news/2008/Vertriebsmeldung_Mai_2008.html.

Question 7

Reference list

BMW (2008). *Corporate News.* Retrieved 22 June 2008, from http://www.bmwgroup.com/e/0_0_www_bmwgroup_com/investor_relations/corporate_news/news/2008/Vertriebsmeldung_Mai_2008.html.

Shamir, B. & Lapidot, Y. (2003). Trust in organizational superiors: Systemic and
    collective considerations. *Organization Studies, 24*(3), 463–491.
Suder, G. (2008). *Doing Business in Europe*. London: Sage.

The reference quiz (part two)

The second part of the quiz will test your learned skills on referencing. It
is highly recommended that you do it to test your knowledge on how to
reference correctly. You will find possible answers in the lists below.
Choose the answer you think is the correct one and enter it into the
appropriate blank space in the following passage. (Hint: Some of the
answer you will not need to use.) Enjoy and good luck!

Nielsen Monitor-Plus, 2003	Hume (1983, as cited inLee & Browne, 1995)	Pitts, Whalen, O'Keefe and Murray's (1989)
(Nielsen Monitor-Plus Reports, 2003)	Friedman and Friedman (1979, as cited in Lee & Browne, 1995)	Pitts, Whalen, O'Keefe & Murray's (1989)
Lee & Browne, 1995	Atkin and Block (1983)	(Qualls, 1989, as cited in Lee & Browne, 1995)
(Lee & Browne, 1995)	Atkin & Block (1983)	(Donohue, Meyer, & Henke, 1978)
(Hume (1990, as cited in Lee & Browne, 1995))	(Atkin & Block, 1983)	(Donohue and Meyer & Henke, 1978)
Hume (1990, as cited in Lee & Browne, 1995)	Friedman & Friedman (1979, as cited in Lee & Browne, 1995)	(Pitts, Whalen, O'Keefe, & Murray's (1989))
Nike, 2004 Nike Company Overview, 2004	Hume (as cited in Lee & Browne, 1995)	Qualls, 1989 (as cited in Lee & Browne, 1995)

The top ten advertisers in the USA spent 12.8 billion dollars in 2002 (US
advertising spending rose nearly 6% in 2002, Nielsen _____). This
represents an increase in advertising expenditure of 10.2% for these companies alone. It is therefore important to evaluate the factors attributable for
the effectiveness of advertising methods, as more than $170 dollars are spent
by the only 12.1% strong African American population (Lee
_____) and the total spending on consumer goods in the USA is
likely to be at least tenfold. This essay thus attempts to look at various

factors that may be accountable for positive and negative consumer responses. The influence advertising, and in particular the use of celebrities as spokespeople, greatly affects consumer spending. Hume (1990_____ Lee_____1995) reports that African Americans are responsible for one-third of Nike's total revenue of $4.7 billion dollars (Nike_____). This product choice is largely influenced by the use of various well-known sports celebrities, such as basketball stars, in ads that are highly renowned among the black American population, and are thought to have a particularly greater impact on black consumer behavior than on white consumer behavior. Hume (1983 _____ Lee & Browne, 1995) states that using celebrities as spokespeople for a brand made a commercial much more believable in the eyes of blacks than commercials abjuring the use of celebrities. Friedman _____ argued that celebrities have an even greater impact on people's perception of a product if it is associated with psychological and social risks. Similar findings are reported by Atkin _____ who argue that the celebrities are seen as a representation for a product rather than as paid spokespeople by young people. As such, a product that is advertised with the help of a celebrity will have a psychological effect with regard to the viewer's belief that this certain product is socially more acceptable, and allows the individual to identify with the celebrity and attempt to follow in his footsteps by obtaining the advertised product. This becomes evident in Pitts_____(1989) observation of African Americans' enthusiasm to ads containing African American symbols, such as Michael Jordan, whereas whites do not appear to show such a strong association pattern (Qualls, 1989_____). This greater impact of celebrity ads on blacks may be due to the fact that children and adolescents from African American households are more likely to spend more time watching television (Donohue_____).

Solution to the reference quiz (part two)

The top ten advertisers in the USA spent 12.8 billion dollars in 2002 (US advertising spending rose nearly 6% in 2002, *Nielsen Monitor-Plus, 2003*). This represents an increase in advertising expenditure of 10.2% for these companies alone. It is therefore important to evaluate the factors attributable for the effectiveness of advertising methods, as more than $170 dollars are spent by the only 12.1% strong African American population (*Lee & Browne, 1995*), and the total spending on consumer goods in the USA is likely to be at least tenfold. This essay thus attempts to look at various factors that may be accountable for positive and negative consumer responses. The influence advertising, and in particular the use of celebrities as spokespeople, greatly affects consumer spending. *Hume (1990, as cited in Lee & Browne, 1995)* reports that African Americans are responsible for one-third of Nike's total revenue of $4.7 billion dollars (*Nike, 2004*). This product choice is largely influenced by the use of various well-known sports celebrities, such as basketball stars, in ads that are highly renowned among the black American population, and are thought to have a particularly greater impact on black consumer behavior than on white consumer behavior. *Hume (1983, as cited in Lee & Browne, 1995)* states that using celebrities as spokespeople for a brand made a commercial much more believable in the eyes of blacks than commercials abjuring the use of celebrities. *Friedman and Friedman (1979, as cited in Lee & Browne, 1995)* argued that celebrities have an even greater impact on people's perception of a product if it is associated with psychological and social risks. Similar findings are reported by *Atkin and Block (1983)* who argue that the celebrities are seen as a representation for a product rather than as paid spokespeople by young people. As such, a product that is advertised with the help of a celebrity will have a psychological effect with regard to the viewer's belief that this certain product is socially more acceptable, and allows the individual to identify with the celebrity and attempt to follow in his footsteps by obtaining the advertised product. This becomes evident in *Pitts, Whalen, O'Keefe and Murray's (1989)* observation of African Americans' enthusiasm to ads containing African American symbols, such as Michael Jordan, whereas whites do not appear to show such a strong association pattern *(Qualls, 1989, as cited in Lee & Browne, 1995)*. This greater impact of celebrity ads on blacks may be due to the fact that children and adolescents from African American households are more likely to spend more time watching television *(Donohue, Meyer & Henke, 1978)*.

Chapter 8

Plagiarism – the Scary Monster

Chapter objectives

Having read this chapter, you will:

- understand what plagiarism is
- know about the different types of plagiarism
- understand how to avoid plagiarism.

How to avoid charges of plagiarism

Most students, when coming to university, are confronted with the term plagiarism at a very early stage. You will have usually heard of it in the first few weeks. Despite it being such an early topic, it still causes a lot of confusion. Let me assure you, it is actually quite straightforward. Let us put it like this: don't use other people's words for your own work by just copying and pasting them. So, to be clear:

DON'T COPY AND PASTE

OK, this isn't quite a hard and fast rule but the only circumstances where you can cut and paste is when you specifically tell the reader that these are not your own words by using quotation marks and then the correct referencing format (see Chapter 6). Although most students don't fall into the trap of plagiarism, some do. The consequences for those who do risk plagiarism are often fatal with regard to their academic career. Punishments for plagiarism are serious, ranging from points being taken off your final work or standing in front of a committee to defend yourself to even getting expelled from university and ending your academic career – at least at that particular institution. This is why it is so important to not risk plagiarism and the easiest way to achieve this is by putting things into your own words. We briefly mentioned in Chapter 6 that one way of avoiding plagiarism is by reading something and then summing it up using your own words, thirty or so seconds later, and giving the reader the necessary reference. Just imagine you want to tell one of your friends about what you have just read. Use your own words to tell this 'imaginary' friend what you are going to use for your essay.

Plagiarism – some examples

There are many types of plagiarism and they are all considered theft of intellectual property:

- handing in an essay written by someone else as your own

- using someone's words, theories, findings, etc. and not giving credit to the author

- using a quote but not putting quotation marks around the quotation to mark it as a quote and adding the correct reference.

So make sure to give credit to the actual author and do not ask any of your friends, boyfriends/girlfriends or anyone else to write the essay for you. Your safest bet, in particular in your first year, is to reference ideas. Don't assume it to be common sense or general knowledge. Everything was once established, explored or theorised by a person, a group of people or an organisation. So don't:

- hand in an essay written by someone else

- 'exchange' parts of essays with others

- copy a web page, parts of a book or article

- give incomplete references.

But do:

- acknowledge the original author by referencing everything you use for your own essay

- paraphrase what you have read

- use your own words and use a reference to say where you have got the idea from

- do use quotation marks where necessary

- give the full reference (see Chapter 6 for how to reference).

One thing we would really like to emphasise is about detection. The most likely reason for students wanting to plagiarise by using other people's work is that they think they won't be caught. In reality, however, cheating (for that is what we are talking about here) is quickly identified by a human marker and plagiarism software is being used by the vast majority of universities these days so your essays are very likely to be scanned electronically for signs of plagiarised content. The same goes for books, articles and other sources. You might be surprised by how many of the books and papers you find in your library are digitalised and can be found online and, therefore, are easily tracked. By any means avoid plagiarism as the consequences will be severe, no matter how little time you have, how bad your notes might be preventing you from identifying the actual source quickly or whatever other reason you might have. Make use of any of the databases out there. They will quickly identify what you are looking for and give you the reference needed, making your essay a clear, safe read.

Let us quickly look at a couple of examples.

Example 1

> Historically, personality tests were not a popular selection tool. They were complex, expensive to train on or would require a psychologist to administer and interpret. The evidence of their criterion validity suggested at best a very modest relationship between test scores on personality tests and work performance.

Sounds good, doesn't it? The knowledge we have on personality tests, nicely put into a critical summary of personality tests. The problem is that these are not really our own words. You might be asking yourself, 'If I did not know these weren't his words, how will a marker know which ones are my own words?' They will, believe me. Markers are quite likely to be lecturers, doctoral researchers and professors who are very familiar with the literature; maybe because they are teaching the subject or it is their research area – or in many cases both.

In order to avoid plagiarism, you need to paraphrase the above text from a textbook by Fincham and Rhodes.

> Fincham and Rhodes (2005) report that due to the costs and difficulties involved in the use of personality tests as a selection tool in, for instance, recruitment and their limited statistical support in predicting work achievement, they failed to be used on a wide scale.

You see what we did to avoid plagiarism? We simply paraphrased the text, keeping the meaning but putting the idea into our own words, and then referenced the source of the information we used for our argument.

If you decide to use part of someone else's work by quoting their idea, you need to use quotation marks. Let's look at the following example.

Example 2

> Knowledge that embraces systems, markets, customers, and new organizational forms has to reflect much more complex realities than the simple provision of a 'product' or 'service'. There is a need to manipulate systems of supply

and distribution, organize the efforts of highly skilled workforces, and command the technologies and methods that can deliver value in the new economy.

Again this is an extract from the textbook written by Fincham and Rhodes. This time we want to use the first sentence word for word, hence quoting Fincham and his colleague.

> Today's successful managers need to be aware that knowledge that embraces systems, markets, customers, and new organizational forms has to reflect much more complex realities than the simple provision of a 'product' or 'service' (Fincham & Rhodes, 2005).

Can you spot what might put you at risk of plagiarising? First we failed to insert quotation marks indicating that we are quoting the authors word for word. Second, the page number is missing, telling the reader exactly where to find the quote.

Therefore, make sure to include these details to stay safe of plagiarism:

> Today's successful managers need to be aware that 'knowledge that embraces systems, markets, customers, and new organizational forms has to reflect much more complex realities than the simple provision of a "product" or "service"' (Fincham & Rhodes, 2005, p. 572).

As long as you follow the referencing guidelines in Chapter 6 and avoid the risks outlined in this chapter, you should be fine and not fall into the 'plagiarism trap'.

Chapter 9

Writing Essays in Exams – Similar But Not the Same

Chapter objectives

By the end of this chapter, you will know:

- the difference between an exam essay and one set as coursework
- how to prepare for exam essays.

You have now read so much about how to plan and write essays, what to watch to create a piece that will earn you best marks and to make sure you do not risk plagiarism. Let us now turn our attention to something you will most likely come across sooner or later in your academic career. Something that confuses a lot of students and frightens them because of the sheer amount to remember: *exam essays*. Yes, the unfortunate fact (for some, however, as other students have told me they actually prefer it over a home assignment) is that some exams require you to write essays. Of course, you have your exams which are multiple choice or ask you to answer a few questions briefly, but, particularly on business courses, you are required to write essays under exam conditions – i.e. answer an essay question using only the information stored in your head. 'Are they any different?' you might be asking yourself. And the answer is yes, slightly.

A few things first: obviously you are less likely to plagiarise, simply due to the fact that you are unlikely to have your book or any other sources with you. Well, you might feel tempted to see what your course mate at the desk next to you is writing. We must warn you, however, as you will see for yourself once entering one of these scary big halls where exams usually take place, there are quite a few invigilators (those people walking around and in the front) standing around to make sure you do not copy your neighbour's thoughts or – in other words – cheat. So your

Table 9.1   Most frequent keywords found in exams

Key word	Meaning
Analyse	Just like in chemistry, break down a concept, for example, into its components and look at them closely.
Apply	Use the concept you are given to describe how it may work in a particular situation.
Compare/contrast	Use two different concepts and look at their similarities and differences.
Define	Explain the meaning of a particular concept.
Discuss	Use a concept and critically look at possible implications (for example, a concept's effects in a particular situation).
Explain	Give reasons why a particular phenomenon may occur or why certain things happen.

best bet (and if you are prepared you should not have any problems) is to tackle any question yourself. But how?

Read the question thoroughly

Yes, as the heading suggests, do read the question thoroughly. Don't just read it once, read it twice, three times – as many times as it takes for you to be entirely sure about what you are asked to write about. You might be surprised how many students do quite badly simply because they fail to answer the question. It can happen so easily that you read something and you misunderstand the question. This could be due to a few reasons. First of all, your memory often plays tricks on you. You might also imagine you are reading something because a question is very similar to something you have prepared or have read before. Sometimes the brain just adds or leaves out words. There are so many different reasons, which is why it is so important that you read the question more than once and that you read it thoroughly. Also, make sure you are absolutely aware of what is being asked of you. Does the question say *discuss, analyse, compare, contrast* or *define*? (See Table 9.1 for an explanation of the different meanings.) Make sure you have fully understood what you are being asked to do. It doesn't matter how much knowledge you have; if you fail to address the question correctly, you will never achieve the top marks you are heading for. So make sure you apply your knowledge exactly to what the question asked you to do.

A few more tips for your successful exam essay are useful here. Don't just jump into writing. We have just established that the first crucial thing in an exam is to read the question carefully, making sure that you understand perfectly. Most exams, however, will contain more than one question. Read through all of them before you decide which to tackle first. It may be that you have to answer all questions or three out of five – any combination is possible. You can use most of the ideas discussed in the chapter on planning (Chapter 2) and you have to remember that the old military adage 'time spent in reconnaissance is seldom wasted' holds true in exams as well as in coursework essays. Actually, it probably applies even more so, since many people panic and don't plan at all in exams. Always have a plan – remember Bear Bryant!

Don't panic!

In exam conditions, many students get very nervous and want to get started as quickly as possible. We remember seeing students starting to write almost before they have turned over the question paper. They may look busy writing but they are most probably 'busy fools' – that is, looking industrious but not really achieving much. The secret of success lies not in rushing, but in your cool and your calmness – your ability to step back and look at the whole sheet in front of you and decide what to tackle first. You are very likely to be nervous going into an exam, and quite understandably so, but if you act cool and pretend that you are calm, it will actually have a calming effect. If you feel the panic starting, put down your pen, close your eyes, breathe slowly in for a count of 20 and then out for a count of 20. Don't repeat this too much or you might fall asleep, but it will have the effect of interrupting the panic voices in your head telling you to rush into answering the exam questions.

The reason behind gaining the advantage of an overall picture is that you will become aware of which questions are easiest to answer; maybe because you are most familiar with the subject, the question is easier to understand, the ideas just keep popping into your head. Whatever it is, focus first on the ones that appear to you the easiest to answer and get started on succeeding in your exam. Only after you have answered those questions that are likely to give you the most success should you start tackling those which appear harder. One important reason for doing it this way around is that once you get to the harder questions you have already experienced a lot of success from answering quite a big chunk of the exam.

Plan your essay

'Planning my essay in an exam?' you might think. Well yes, we advise you to develop an outline of what you want to write. Just as you would do for an essay you write at home or in the computer lab, don't just jump into writing. You need to make a plan functioning as a map, guiding you through the essay. Only a plan, an outline, a map – whatever you want to call it – will enable you to write this masterpiece, getting you the good and top mark you are heading for. Since you are reading this book, we are pretty sure you are one of those students who prepares really well for an exam. Doing the outline will help you to recall the things you have learned and read. You will be surprised how much your memory can store. Not only will planning your essay help you to write your essay, but it will also help your memory to activate the stored knowledge. It is a simple process. By writing down keywords and developing a plan, your memory can use those words to tap into your knowledge. You can easily try it by just writing a few keywords down and then see how many things you can remember. You will be surprised how much you actually know. The outline of your essay simply helps you to put everything in order.

Before getting started on the written outline of your essay, keep in mind that you only have a limited amount of time for each question, so make sure to incorporate time restrictions in your plan. If you have 4 questions and 2 hours to do the exam, then calculate about 30 minutes per question. Obviously if there are questions you think you might not be able to write much on, then adjust your allocated time accordingly. This is all part of the bird's eye view you should have by now when looking at the exam questions. If you are not sure yet how much time and how much knowledge you have on each question, then take another overall look. Believe me, though this all sounds like a lot of work, it will be worth it. Planning your exam questions might take you maybe 15 or 20 minutes, but these 15 or 20 minutes are well spent.

The outline

Before looking at some examples, we want to let you in on a little secret. You don't need to scribble stuff on the desk! Just ask for an additional piece of paper to draw up your essay plan. The invigilators will be more than happy to supply you with blank paper you can use for your essay outline. Or you can just use the answer book and put a line through it. We have never come across universities who penalise students for this. Also, exam time is not a time to be concerned about how much paper you are using. It may not be all that green but use as much paper as you need – paper is of course a sustainable resource so it isn't all that environmentally unfriendly to do this! Cramming things onto a small space might actually interfere with your train of thought and will, of course, make it more difficult to mark – and you want to make it easy for the marker to give you those marks you have worked so hard to achieve. Once you have got the paper, there are different ways of creating the map that will guide you through your exam essay. Just see what works best for you. Let us look at a sample exam question below.

Discuss the effects of political decisions on corporate performance.

Now you have done all your reading and your head is just full of ideas. First thing to do, put them all down on paper to make sense of them and to get them into order. The last thing you want to do when sitting an

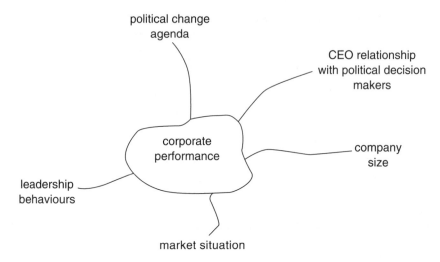

Figure 9.1   Planning an exam essay using a diagram

exam is to be halfway through your essay and then remember something really important you should have put into the middle section. Remember, an exam essay is handwritten. The wonderful gadgets you get with any word processor – allowing you to move things around – are of no use now. This is why it is so important to plan your essay and allocate the next 30 or 60 minutes as clearly as possible. Among many other things you can do, here are two examples of methods which you can use to plan your essay: draw a diagram (see Figure 9.1) or make a list (see Figure 9.2).

Go with whatever you feel most suits you. You could alternatively use the diagram to brainstorm and create a table or list plan to do the specific essay planning. As you can see in Figure 9.2, the list consists of two parts: the introduction and the main body. You do not really need an outline for the conclusion as an essay develops and you will see what best comprises your conclusion once the introduction and your main body have been written.

For each part, list what you want to say in the appropriate order and list who said what next to the points. Try also to put them into an order so all you have to do when writing your essay is go by the outline you have created. You can see these arrows pointing, labelled *List references,* to the right of the list. This is a very helpful thing to do. Not only write down what you want to say in terms of facts, aspects, findings, etc. but also write down who said, found or claimed what and in what year. Look at the outline as a map which guides you from start to finish.

Write your essay

Now you have prepared your outline, you should have a very good idea what to write. If you don't, then go back again. Writing without planning

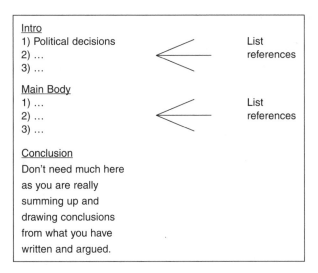

Figure 9.2   Planning an exam essay using a list

is likely to lead to massive problems. Writing in an exam, however, is slightly different from writing a home essay. The lecturer or marker of your exam will not expect you to present information in as detailed a form as in a home assignment. You are not expected to be able to give the exact reference for a quote. For most people, remembering a particular quote among all the other things you will have to learn for your exam is very difficult. The same applies to the exact dates. Don't worry if you cannot remember a particular date. No one will mark you down for writing 'Smith (1981)' instead of the correct 'Smith (1982)', for example. The main thing is that you actually remember that the person you are mentioning actually did develop a particular theory. As an example, don't write 'Fincham and Rhodes (2004) state in their motivation theory that people are motivated by different needs'. You may well have read this in a book which has the authors Fincham and Rhodes on the cover, but it isn't their theory. In contrast to what we have said about coursework essays, it is not necessary that you tell the examiner that you found Maslow's theory in a particular textbook. You therefore do not need to say 'cited in'. It is much more important that you remember that the hierarchy of needs theory was developed by Abraham Maslow and is usually attributed to the year 1954. So write:

According to Maslow's (1954) hierarchy of needs, people strive to fulfil different levels of needs.

But let us now look at some guidelines you can use for your exam answers. First of all, just as you would do in a normal essay, start with an overview of what you will be talking about and define important concepts. There is no need to spend half a page on this, just a couple of sentences telling the reader where you are going is enough. This also emphasises to the examiner that you have thought about the structure of your essay and know what you are talking about. One thing upfront: as in a regular essay, do not ramble. Think of your examiner as someone who will probably have to mark over a hundred – or even more – exam papers so the secret in this context is that you are detailed, specific and you stick to what is important. Also make sure – and your essay plan should do this for you – that you stay on a particular path, giving your essay a good flow. Don't talk about motivation, then leadership, then performance, only then to jump back to motivation. Make sure your exam essay is structured smoothly, just as you would if you were at home typing away. Again, at no point are you expected to be as precise as you would be with a home piece, and mistakes regarding dates and even names which are similar will be forgiven. One important aspect, however, is time. When writing an essay at home, you can usually take as much time as you want to finish a good piece. An exam, by its very nature, is very different. So keep the clock in mind. By no means are we telling you to constantly look at the clock, but be aware of time restrictions. Set yourself a particular frame in which you allow yourself to answer a question, making sure you have enough time for the other questions.

I have forgotten something

At times you will happily write and be well on your way to writing this perfect piece to get you a great mark when something really important pops into your head – something you need to include to make this essay even stronger. If this aspect is not directly related to what you are writing just at that given moment, make a quick note on your outline and finish putting your current thought on paper. It is important that you do note down whatever has just come to mind, as you are likely to forget it. Your brain is occupied with writing, and recalling and storing new information is of a much lesser priority. Once you have finished what you wanted to say, get back to your outline and see where exactly your new idea, the theory or the finding will fit in. If it happens that you have already written the part that this new idea should be incorporated into, then there are a couple of things you can do. If there is some space, or if your additional point is not too long, try and add it somewhere near where it should go by simply writing it down. A lot of times, however, in particular if your addition is a few sentences, mark the location where it should go with a star or a number and write your thought down on the top or bottom of the page or an additional sheet. However you do it, make sure it is as clear as possible and your remarks are as neat as possible. Make absolutely sure that the examiner can locate which part of your essay your additional comment belongs to.

Finishing off your essay

Make sure that you leave time for proofreading. Whether you do this just after finishing the essay or at the end of your exam is up to you. Whatever works best for you. Usually, however, it helps to gain some distance from your work. Even though you are unable to leave a couple of days as you should when writing an essay at home, the time spent answering the other questions might have given you some of the necessary time and cognitive distance needed to look at your essay more objectively. It is also very likely to help you just to put down your pen for two minutes, look around and only then get back to reading what you have written. This will help your brain to relax and will give you some of the necessary freshness to be more objective when proofreading your essays. A few things to watch out for when proofreading.

- Is your essay clean and neat or did you scribble all over the place?

- Is your essay nicely structured: introduction, main body with structured and coherent paragraphs, does the conclusion sum up and fit the requirements of the question?

- Does your essay look pretty much as you planned it?

It may be that you come across something that does not make as much sense as you originally thought. Cross it out neatly – don't turn half the page blue or black. Always keep in mind that the person marking your essay is a human being and likely to be affected by the presentation of your essay. If you need to add something, do it with the stars and numbers as described above. If you need to change something around, also use a number and indicate to the reader that a particular part follows on further down and not immediately, for example. Once you are happy with it and if you still have some spare minutes, sit back, have a look around and read your answers again just to make absolutely sure. If you are happy, hand in your exam and relax – you have done it.

Advanced exam essay-writing skills

As with all the other advanced skills sections, you must get the basics right before attempting this section. We have suggestions for both the preparation for the exam and writing of your essays in exam conditions.

- Preparation – learn specific theories including dates.
- Writing – full plan, perfectly executed, finishing exactly on time.

Preparation

There is an old piece of military wisdom which is:

Preparation and planning prevents poor performance.

(Continued)

(Continued)

This is particularly true for exams where you need to focus a long time in advance of the exam date. The aim is that, when you walk into the exam room, you are as relaxed and confident as it is possible to be given the rather stressful nature of exams. Of course, you will never be completely happy at the prospect of an exam we realise! So in your planning you start with the exam week and work backwards, taking account of all the other commitments you have (lectures, reading, socialising, sport, work, phoning your mum, and so on) and work out your revision plan for each exam. For exams which require essays, the key piece of advice stems from understanding the rules of the game. You cannot be an expert in all the topics covered in a module – and it is very rare that lecturers expect you to be. Most module exams will contain some form of choice about which questions to answer and getting a very good understanding of how the lecturer has designed the assessment is essential even to pass well. To go beyond the pass level, you need to be completely on top of the material needed for the exam. If you know which topics you need to learn for the exam, you can devote your attention to learning them in detail. We recommend that for each topic you identify the key theories and learn them inside out. Make sure you can cite the name and date of the theory, and also know the key criticisms of each one and even who the critics are. For some topics, this could mean one central theory which could be applied to most questions but you also need to have more than a working knowledge of the lesser theories too. The main difference between a good exam essay and a great one, in terms of content, is whether or not the student is able to reproduce the precise theory required as well as answering the question set. It is rote learning, which is generally frowned on these days but is absolutely essential if you are going for a high mark in a closed book exam.

Writing

For advanced writing in exams, you should follow most of the advice given about advanced writing for coursework – check back for that now if you haven't read it already. One additional critical point in exams is this:

MANAGE YOUR TIME PROPERLY

You need to be completely aware of how long you have for each question you are writing and be ruthless in stopping work on a question when you reach the time allocation. So often we see students whose first exam essay is brilliant but then they have not got the time to answer the rest of the questions properly. Don't get carried away when you see the question you can really nail. Allow time for the ones you are less sure of because they will actually take longer for you to work out answers to. Perhaps most importantly, allow yourself time to plan your work. Do not allow yourself to dive straight in and start writing too soon. Always take stock, work out skeleton answers to questions before starting to write. If there aren't too many questions, one trick is to work out answers to all the questions before you start any. You will often be surprised that when you do this the obvious question might not be the best one to choose. If you look at the paper and perhaps think you can only answer one question (even after sketching out answers), just start on the one you can answer and very often the way to answer the others will come to you.

Almost all texts about exams recommend leaving time to check your work and ours is no exception. However, we have often seen students who spot mistakes which either are not mistakes at all (then they change the answer and lose the marks) or there isn't time to correct the mistakes anyway. Yes, allow yourself five minutes to check for clarity but allocate more time to the planning stage before you start writing your essay. Once you are into an essay, it is really difficult to start again or to change questions, so make sure you choose carefully. This brings us neatly back to the point we started this section with:

Preparation and planning prevents poor performance.

Chapter 10

Motivation – How to Keep Going When it Gets Tough

Chapter objectives

Having read this chapter, you will:

- understand how to take care of your basic needs before you start
- start thinking about your personal learning style
- integrate ideas of planning into your personal style
- have reflected on why you are at university and have some ideas about how to get the best out of your time there.

Sometimes essay writing can feel like a bit of a battle. Fighting your way through textbooks, journals and websites trying to build a convincing argument isn't easy – and, frankly, there are probably dozens of things you'd rather do. Still, essay writing is an important part of the academic experience which helps you to develop some of the key skills you need to have when you enter the workforce. Also, as many of the assessments set as part of your degree requirement involve essay writing, you'll actually need to master the art if you want to do well on your course. Of course, knowing *how* to write good essays is only one part of essay writing success – the other and equally important element is *actually writing* good essays! This means that you will need to know how to motivate yourself, which – as we all know – isn't always easy. That's why we've decided to use this chapter to show how you can manage your motivation levels and give you the extra push you need to complete the work.

We've all been there. Sitting in your room or the library with the laptop in front of you, staring at the screen, blank expression on your face, wishing that the words would just appear, switching between e-mail and Facebook, and wondering what the others are doing tonight. Whatever your preferred distraction is, it's likely that it'll come into your mind when you're writing an essay. If you are at home, even the most boring chore suddenly seems vitally important – 'I can't start writing until the washing-up is done' or 'It really is about time that the freezer was defrosted'. Then there is the addiction that is daytime TV! In the library, there are always friends to catch up with, coffee to drink, newspapers to read. The list of distractions is nearly endless! We can't take these distractions away but we can see if we can help you to overcome them a little in this chapter.

Essay writing demands a lot of thinking and the use of intellect, so isn't something you can just do on the hop (at least not if you want to do it well!) or when you're demotivated, because you're thinking about all the other things you'd rather do or because you don't know if you are doing the right sort of work. You could also be stressed – because you can't concentrate and the deadline is moving closer – when writing the essay can feel like climbing a mountain. Where to start? What to do? The problem is that once you're demotivated and stressed, writing actually becomes much more difficult (hence the importance of the preparation discussed in Chapter 2).

In this chapter, we discuss some of the common demotivators students encounter and offer some advice on how successfully to manage yourself and get the work done. We begin by talking about the importance of ensuring the basic needs are met, so you can avoid unnecessary distraction and focus completely on the task at hand. In addition, we discuss ways you can identify what motivates you and give you some tricks on how to keep your motivation high.

More pressing needs

Why can't you focus? Well, it could be because there is something else demanding your focus and distracting your attention. How do you avoid these types of issues? In line with many core motivation theories (e.g. Maslow, 1954), we suggest you start by ensuring that your basic needs are satisfied. Basic needs comprise physical, social and psychological needs and by keeping these needs balanced you will be able to focus your energies entirely on the task at hand – in this case essay writing.

Physical (financial)

First things first! If you are thinking about how to put your next meal on your table or where you're going to sleep at night, you won't be able to focus on writing an essay (indeed, it will seem like the least of your worries). Although the scenario we have just described is an extreme case, we are aware that many students face some financial difficulties. You need some financial resources to sustain yourself and satisfy your basic needs for food, drink, shelter. Money does matter. If you find yourself in a financially difficult situation, we suggest you try to resolve it by seeking out help and advice. Most (if not all) universities offer support services, which students can use confidentially and free of charge. Examples include tutors, advisers and support teams (e.g. personal tutor, international student office, specific student advice functions, chaplains, etc). Inform yourself and get in touch with the most appropriate person or persons. And, remember, there is no shame in asking for advice. In fact, it often takes a lot more courage to face up to your situation and ask for help than simply ignoring the problem and hoping it will go away somehow. If you are in a difficult situation, universities may also be able to help you administratively, for instance allowing for extensions on coursework due to extenuating circumstances.

Another way to ensure that your physical needs are satisfied is by staying physically active. We know that it's often easier said than done and that the last thing you'll want to do with a 5,000-word essay hanging over your head is to 'waste' an hour at the gym, but physical exercise is actually critical and should be integrated into everyone's routine. Apart from helping you stay healthy, it also has other positive effects. For instance, it helps stimulate mental activity and, believe it or not, actually increases your energy and motivation levels! It doesn't take a lot to achieve these positive effects. Even 30 minutes of physical exercise every day are sufficient to draw benefit from the activity. Try it, you might actually enjoy it! And if you feel like you need an extra push, take a friend with you to help keep you going.

Social (relational)

The academic life can sometimes feel lonely, especially during periods when you are spending countless hours alone in the library collating reference material and/or putting together a coherent argument in the solitary confinement of your room. Some people, especially those with a strong social drive, find individual coursework a real challenge because it takes them out of their comfort zone by removing them from the social arena. If you are this type of person, you're unlikely to find essay writing very motivating and may even become glum at the very prospect. Of course this only acts to compound motivational problems and drag out the essay-writing process. We suggest you build social activities into your work (e.g. study groups, joint library trips, mutual reviews and editing work) and also ensure you keep socially active throughout your degree. Join some clubs and societies, and reward yourself with some social interaction after you have completed your work.

Apart from being a lot of fun, social activities are actually incredibly important in a number of ways. They provide an opportunity to balance your working life by giving you a chance to take a break from the work. Talking to others is also a good way to share your experience with peers, gain new insights by viewing issues from a different perspective and get advice on topics you find difficult to understand. Also, if you are new at university and haven't quite managed to find your feet in the social arena, there is always your family! They can also be an important source of emotional support and get you to reflect on the situation from a new perspective.

A word of caution though – don't join so many societies that you get distracted from your work. These days it costs you and your family an enormous amount of money to go to university so make sure you are getting the best value out of your time. Students are often encouraged to think of the cost of education in terms of investment so when you make your decisions about how you spend your time, you should think of it in terms of where you are making your investment. Is it in activities which will pay off?

Psychological (emotional)

Your time at university will be full of ups and downs – academically, emotionally and physically. This is part of the learning experience but can also take its toll, especially if it seems that the downs are starting to outweigh the ups! University is generally something that takes place for many students during the identity formation years, which means that the process will have a huge impact on your life and you need to ensure that this impact is positive. So it is important that you also remember to take care of your mental welfare. No matter what it may look like from the outside, everyone struggles at one point or another; it's just a natural part of the growth process. It often helps to openly talk about your experiences, as it makes you realise that you're not alone. Most of the time talking to your friends or family will be enough to get you through but if things do ever get to be too much, there are other people you can talk to. For instance, you can seek confidential advice from advisers, counsellors or psychologists. It doesn't have to be anything formal, it could just be a friendly chat; most university services operate an open door policy, which allows you to drop in whenever you feel the need. Actually you will very often find that other people are really struggling too and perhaps just putting on an organised front. When you find that others have the same problems as you, it is often a huge relief and also you can pull together to find ways round things. This might not be in study groups but just allowing time to vent your frustrations and hear other people's can be a great release of tension.

What type of learner are you?

Everyone is different and this is also true when it comes to learning and learning styles. Students learn in different ways and have different needs when it comes to method, location and time; so it is crucial that you figure out what works best for you. If you know how you can work best, you can take advantage of your personal strengths and become efficient in your work – and we all know that less is more, right? Most students actually don't know how they learn best when they come to university, which means that they have to invest some time in finding out how they can motivate themselves and do well. You can do this in a number of ways but the best way is often to try out diverse ways of working. At the same time remember that you may need to find a variety of ways of working, as some ways of working are better suited to certain times or tasks – in short, there is no 'one size fits all' solution. What works in one size situation may not work in another! Keep this in mind when reviewing different ways of working.

When trying out different methods, consider the following factors:

- the work environment: the setting you are working in:
  - o   for example, office, library, study room, bedroom, kitchen
- the conditions: the conditions you are working in:
  - o   for example, noise level, lighting, location in the room, people around you, background distractions like music or TV
- the task: the assignment you are working on:
  - o   for example, preparing for an exam essay, doing a comparative essay, offering a description or evaluation
- the method: the technique you are using to do the work:
  - o   for example, structured, unstructured, individual or group sessions
- the timing: the time of day when you are trying to do the work:
  - o   morning, afternoon, evening; early on or close to the deadline.

When considering how you work best, evaluate the various techniques on the basis of four general factors:

- speed: how quickly you work
- persistence: how long you are able to persist at the task (how many breaks you need)
- quality: how well you've done the work
- enjoyment: how much you enjoy working this way.

We all know that it's not enough to do an assignment quickly; you also have to do it well if you want to succeed on your course. Persistence and enjoyment are closely linked – if you hate the way you're working, even if you're efficient and produce good-quality work, you are unlikely to persist at it very long.

Motivational problems

There are a number of issues that can act as demotivators when it comes to essay writing, such as:

- workload
- lack of direction

- repetitiveness of the task
- boredom
- distractions
- fear of failure.

We'll go through these one by one, explaining both what the problem is and how you can address it effectively.

Workload

One of the most common issues for undergraduates is that they struggle with the workload. They are not used to autonomous working as the previous learning environments they have come from tend to be much more structured, with the information being fed to them rather than them being required to seek out and comprehend information themselves. University is a big step up and sometimes students just don't know where to start. So much to do in so little time (and you first have to learn the skills to actually be able to do what's being asked of you). It can all get to be a bit much and, even when you're working hard, sometimes can feel like you're treading water and getting nowhere. This can be very demotivating.

What can you do? You can make the task less daunting in a number of ways including breaking the task down, engaging in backward planning and creating information linkages. Each is discussed in turn below.

Break the task down

Human capacity for information is limited – people can only process between five and nine pieces of information at any one time (Miller, 1956). As it is difficult for us to work with more than nine items of information in our mental space, one technique commonly cited to facilitate work is to break the task down. Essays become more manageable when they are chunked into goals and sub-goals. This also helps you to structure your task and make a plan for how you are going to achieve it. Goal setting is actually also a very good way to give yourself a direction. This can be challenging, especially when you're starting out. Remember that good goals are challenging and specific (Locke, 1968). See below for more advice on planning and goal setting.

Backward planning

Backward planning is a method of planning which endorses fixing an end goal and then starting to plan your work backwards from that end goal.

So if you want to submit your essay to the coursework office by the deadline date, you'll first need to (in reverse order): print the essay, type it, proofread it, build a coherent argument, do the background research, prepare an essay plan, choose your general approach and choose a topic (in the case that one is not provided for you). Since none of the stages can be achieved without the preceding stage, it gives you a comprehensive idea of the necessary steps towards the end goal, in this case submitting an essay in time for the deadline. You then start allocating time and planning your tasks based on the deadline. If you need to submit your deadline by Day X, say, you know that you need to print off your essay by Day X, which means you will already have built a coherent argument, which takes X days ... and so on. Continue planning this way until you reach the first stage of essay writing. Whichever day your calculation falls on is the latest day that you need to begin the process. Using this method not only allows you to work your way through the process but it also allows you to break down the task *and* set yourself deadlines, which are important in order for you to monitor your progress.

Creating information linkages

During your degree you will be confronted with a lot of new information, not all of which you will be able to commit to memory instantly – unless you have a photographic memory, with which only very few of us are blessed. So what do you do? Cheat! By associating new material with existing knowledge, you will make it easier to remember the material – thereby giving yourself a clear advantage. For instance, if you're a modern languages student writing an essay about the impact of the Gujarati language on Indian businesses and you are trying to learn the Gujarati letter B (બ), it will be easier to commit to memory if you remind yourself that the symbol looks like a sideways B. This way you are actually associating new knowledge with already existing schemata, thereby simplifying the thought process by making it less strenuous. Another good example is the use of abbreviations. For instance, if you are studying business and psychology, you might have used the acronym OCEAN (openness, conscientiousness, extraversion, agreeableness and neuroticism) to summarise the big five personality factors (cf. McCrae & Costa, 1990). If you have a difficult time remembering, then these are legitimate ways of tricking your mind into being more efficient.

Lack of direction

An additional issue for undergraduate students when writing essays is to decide in which direction to take an essay. This is especially true where there is some choice in topics or takes you can have on a topic. This choice all too often translates into ambiguity and uncertainty for students, who want to do the best they can but aren't sure what that means or how they achieve it. This means that a lot of learning takes place, evident through personal growth, but it also means that it is associated with feelings of discomfort and anxiety.

What can you do? A few good ways to resolve the issue is to ask peers, to ask advisers, to consult the literature and to do a few trial runs.

Asking peers

If you are having difficulty setting your own goals or deciding in which direction to take your essay, talk to others. Get feedback on your ideas, sound them out and see what others think. This can be very helpful, by relieving some of the anxiety and speeding the process up. Instead of wasting hours going around in circles, you have a point of departure that you can move on from. However, you need to be careful not to rely on others too much – at university you need to produce independent work, so it's important that you only seek clarification, not take others' ideas and pass them off as your own.

Asking advisers

An alternative avenue is to ask your adviser, lecturer or tutor for advice. Discuss some of your ideas with them and see if that is what they're looking for. If the set question is a little ambiguous, it's OK to ask for clarification to ensure you're moving in the right direction. This is best done in the planning stages to avoid unnecessary reworking. Besides, lecturers will only very rarely agree to read your work – otherwise it would give you an unfair advantage over your peers and take away from your learning process.

Consulting the literature

When in doubt READ. Reading your core text or introductory journal articles on a topic can be very helpful in giving you ideas about how to move the essay forward. There are lots of different approaches to essay writing and topics, so reading is a good way to broaden your horizon and increase your awareness of the literature at the same time.

Trial runs

If you're still not sure about the best way to approach the essay, make a couple of essay plans. See which works best for the topic and which gives you the most satisfactory result. Using this technique you can be sure you've tried your best to find the right approach and also increase the learning that takes place by exposing yourself to different literature and ideas.

Repetitiveness of the task

Although doing a degree is an intellectual journey, the work sometimes feels very repetitious. Reading book after book, paper after paper and then writing, writing, writing can be very exhausting and become dull over time. Repetition can be a recipe for success, though, as it reinforces the learning that has taken place, all the while feeding you with new information and bringing about new ideas. So to all intents and purposes, practice makes perfect. However, unfortunately, monotony can often also drive out the enthusiasm and lead to demotivation.

What can you do? You can make repetitive tasks more enjoyable and less demotivating by increasing variety, engaging in forward thinking, improving the task, breaking the task down and using the repetitive elements of the work as a distraction task.

Increasing variety

Intellectual work demands a lot of concentration, which is strenuous and may mean that you have to discipline yourself to continue. You can improve your attention span by introducing variation into your work. Why don't you try varying your work? Switch back and forth between tasks when you notice that you're becoming fatigued. If that doesn't work (if you are one of those students who hates multi tasking), try to trick your mind into believing the work is more interesting than it is. Add some stimulation, for example playing some music in the background, or change work settings to give yourself a short mental break.

Engaging in forward thinking

Another good trick is to use forward thinking. While writing your essay, think about all the nice things you'll be able to do once you're done and always remind yourself of the superordinate goals of what you're trying to achieve – getting an A on the essay or getting a good degree – as this will help to keep you motivated.

Improving the task

If you don't find the essay topic interesting, you can improve the task by adding another dimension to it. Try thinking about how the topic of the essay connects with those things you have a real interest in – or try to make the activities more fun. For instance, you can log the sources you consult into a database and do basic frequency counts on them or group them into different types of papers. This will take a little longer but will help focus your attention and increase your efficiency!

Breaking the task down

As already discussed earlier in this section, another thing you can do is break the task down. Reducing the task into its constituent elements will make it more manageable and easier to complete. For instance, you can set yourself the goal of reading one or two papers a day or consulting two books every week. If you are not enjoying the work, forcing yourself to do it all in one go won't help. Breaking the task down will keep you efficient, making you more effective in the long term and helping you to avoid simple errors.

Using distraction tasks

If you have reached a stage that you find very difficult, whether it be consulting the literature or proofreading, then how about using it as a break from more challenging and enjoyable work. Think of these tasks as distraction tasks in their own right to stimulate other work you're doing, whether this is another piece of coursework, studying for an exam or preparing for a tutorial.

Boredom

Boredom. We know it all too well. You find something mindnumbing and can't focus on it. It has to be done, but you wish it wouldn't have to be done by you! Boredom strikes everyone – even us academics (!) – and that is because human beings have a limited capacity to pay attention. Attention span differs from person to person and depends on the situation they find themselves in, but studies suggest that the average attention span in adults is between 15 and 20 minutes (Johnstone & Percival, 1976). To make matters worse, our attention reduces over time and can fall to three or four minutes after an extensive period of effort.

What can you do? If you feel your attention waning, try taking breaks.

Taking breaks

Get up, walk around the room and allow yourself to focus again. Take regular breaks, including decent lunch breaks (see above about physical needs) and don't work long hours – not only will you be far less efficient, you'll also be unhappy. Also have at least one day off per week. At university the work you get assigned is continuous, so there is always something you could be doing, but, if you've been working hard, reward yourself with some time off. Your mind needs it to recuperate. How about using it as an opportunity to get in that exercise you've been promising yourself?

Distractions

Distractions are everywhere. There is always something you'd rather do than work. This is especially true if you have ended up with an essay topic that doesn't stimulate your interests and you find it a real chore.

What can you do? Again, a number of techniques are available to help you circumvent distractions. For instance, you can remove the distractions or engage in behavioural self-management.

Remove the distractions

If you are prone to becoming distracted, the best thing you can do is to remove yourself from the environment where the distractions are present. If you're doing something dull and are having a difficult time concentrating on the task at hand, any distraction will do! If you find it hard not to turn the TV on when you know your favourite show is on (but you also know you should be working), try going to the library or to the park to work. Make your life easier by removing the temptation altogether.

Behavioural self-management

Behavioural self-management is actually a formal method to avoid distraction (Luthans & Davis, 1979). According to this method, it is important to recognise and boundary undesirable behaviour. It suggests choosing a learning environment, which triggers the desired behaviour. Pick a learning spot and stick to it – that way your mind will, over time, become conditioned to the idea of 'learning' in this space and thus reducing the effort it takes for you to get going. One of the ways you can shape your behaviour positively is by reinforcing desirable behaviour. You can easily achieve this through reward. Every time you reach a milestone or achieve a task, give yourself a little present. That could be something tangible (like a pair of jeans!) or something intangible (like some time with friends). People also use punishment and deprival to eliminate negative behaviours, which means that they forbid themselves to do something because they haven't achieved the set out targets or objectives. Reward is actually a more powerful motivator than punishment, so we suggest you treat yourself!

Fear of failure

'I don't know if I can do it' is a sentence we've heard hundreds of times from students. Being an undergraduate isn't easy, with so much social and intellectual learning going on, it's not hard to become overwhelmed.

The bottom line is this – if you weren't clever enough to be at university, you wouldn't have been admitted in the first place. You CAN do it; you may just need a little push.

What can you do? There is only one thing you can really do: keep trying.

Try, try and try again

The easiest way to fail is by not trying, so do the best you can do. Remember that the British education system accounts for the adjustment period students go through when they first come to university by allocating a lower percentage of the overall degree grade to the first and second years than to the final year. You have some room for error and time to grow. Take advantage of it!

Remember why you're at university

We conclude this chapter with some food for thought. Degrees aren't easy – otherwise everyone would have one. You can't expect to go through a degree course without experiencing any difficulties and difficulties open the door for discouragement and demotivation. When you are going through this type of phase, remember that it's just that – a phase! There will be ups and downs but in the end you'll pull through and be stronger for it. It's the journey, the overall learning experience – emotionally and intellectually – that really matters. And, of course, it helps to call to mind why you're writing the essay in the first place. Where does it fit into the overall picture? Well, it's part of your module requirement, course requirement and degree requirement. At the end, when you've written your essays successfully, you will stand there on the final day of your three- or four-year degree course – surrounded by friends and family – and can be really really proud of yourself and your achievements. And what did it start with? One terribly frustrating essay that, in the end, you managed to pull off because you knew how important it was. Also remember that the degree is only part of your journey. Think about the contributions you will make in your careers, when you're a CEO, foreign exchange dealer or a HR director, a consultant or a lecturer (or even organic farmer, tepee seller or flower arranger). In the end we think you'll agree that the journey was well worth it.

References

Fincham, R. and Rhodes, P. (2005) *Principles of Organisational Behaviour.* Oxford: Oxford University Press.

Johnstone, A.H. and Percival, F. (1976) Attention breaks in lectures. *Education in Chemistry, 13*(2): 49–50.

Locke, E.A. (1968) Toward a theory of task motivation and incentives. *Organizational Behaviour and Human Performance*, 3: 157–89.

Luthans, F. and Davis, T.R. (1979) Behavioral self-management – The missing link in managerial effectiveness. *Organizational Dynamics*, *8*(1): 42–60.

Maslow, A.H. (1954) *Motivation and Personality*. New York: Harper.

McCrae, R.R. and Costa, P.T. (1990) *Personality in Adulthood*. New York: Guilford.

Miller, G. (1956) The magic number 7+2. *Psychological Review*, *63*(2): 81–97.

Appendix 1
Example Questions and How to Answer Them

Here are some examples of essays which are fairly typical of those set in a number of subjects at university. We have given you a quick idea how to tackle each one.

Question 1 What is the relationship between personality and creativity?

You need to define the terms and show you know the literature they came from and then show in what way they are related. So you would probably open with a definition of personality and then describe what the main theories say about it. Then do the same for creativity. You should pick the theories in each case which will show at least some overlap but allow you some opportunity to show differences too – but this is only an ideal.

Question 2 Consider ways in which government influences business and vice versa.

A fairly standard question which is asking you to show both directions of the influence linkage. If you only show that government influences business, you will probably fail. The best answers will show well-evidenced ways in which government influences business and then do the same for business influencing government. The question doesn't ask you to come to a conclusion which way is more prevalent but it would be an idea to draw a brief conclusion from your evidence showing you have balanced the arguments and come to a conclusion. Don't emphasise this too much though because the question doesn't ask you to do it!

Question 3 'The position of trade unions has, in the United Kingdom, been utterly transformed since the 1980s, and not only by legislation.' Discuss.

First you need to show the ways in which trade unions have changed since the 1980s with appropriate evidence. Then you would probably go on to describe some ways in which they have changed because of legislation and consider other ways in which they have been made to change. Your overall conclusion would be to summarise these ways.

Question 4 What is the motivation in the long run for firms to engage in limit pricing?

First you define 'limit pricing' showing that you not only know what it is but also the names of the key researchers. Then you consider ways in which firms would want to use this but make sure you stick to long-term issues because that is what the question asks you to do.

Question 5   Explain the role of human capital as determinant of economic growth.

You would probably open with a general description of the various influences on economic growth – including human capital. Then you would move on to explain where human capital sits among the other influences. Your conclusions would restate the influences you show during the essay.

Question 6   To what extent do national and organisational cultures affect creativity? How can a culture for innovation be fostered? Provide examples to illustrate your answer.

This question has several parts to it and you must make sure you answer all of them – miss any out and you run the risk of failing. In your plan we suggest you write each of them on a different line with some notes about what you are going to say about each next to them. Start with defining national culture, then organisational culture. Discuss the overlaps between the two concepts. Move on to define innovation, then pull together the ideas of national and organisational cultures together with those of innovation. Finally, make sure you provide some examples for each of your main points – the question asks for all of this so make sure you provide all of these elements. Although this is a complicated question, it does tell you precisely what you have to do, so follow it very closely.

Question 7   Evaluate the organisational issues associated with recruitment and selection and other HRM policies and practices in relation to either:
a)   impression management, or
b)   managing diversity.

This is a very specific question which you need to read very carefully before planning your answer. The key elements are recruitment, selection and any other HRM policy/practice and how these relate to either (a) or (b). So first you need to check that you have enough to say on all these areas before you decide to tackle the question. If this were a coursework question, you would tailor your reading to either topic (a) or (b) and perhaps also look for useful ways to find what other HRM policies and practices you might include. Since policy and practice are both mentioned in the question, you would be well advised to include both in your answer.

Question 8   'The career is dead, long live the career!' Discuss.

This question could come under the heading of 'hardy perennial' – that is, it frequently crops up on courses covering careers. There is very little to go on in the question which makes it actually quite hard to answer. If you are confronted with this in an exam, you need to be really confident that you can provide a good answer before choosing it. The more specific questions (i.e. ones where you can see exactly what the examiner wants you to do) are in most cases easier to answer well. We would approach this question by describing the various models and theories about careers, then move on to discuss why the career has changed so in some ways we don't have a career in the way we used to. Then move on to talk about what the modern career is. Make sure that you have 'discussed' the statement though, by going into detail why the statement has value (or not). Make sure that your answers to such questions are not really dumping on paper all you know on a subject – that sort of approach will not gain you any marks!

Question 9   Explain the key components of integrated marketing communications. Also discuss their suitability in the promotion mix using AIDA model.

A very targeted question where you need to just follow what the question asks you to do. First explain/describe the key components of Integrated Marketing Communications, then describe the Promotion Mix and the AIDA model. Finally discuss the suitability aspect of the question. Cover all these points well and you must gain good marks.

Appendix 2

General Undergraduate Marking Scheme

Example undergraduate marking scheme

As used at Aston University (reproduced with permission).

1st (>80%) An outstanding achievement for an undergraduate with regard to analysis, interpretation, synthesis, evaluation and presentation. Such work is likely to discuss issues rarely identified by undergraduates and may, for example, exhibit a novelty of approach distinguishing it from work within the 70–79% range. No irrelevant material. Referencing correct. No (or only minor) errors in spelling and/or grammar.	
1st (70–79%) Excellent grasp of knowledge, with evidence of wide reading and/or research, analysed in depth to support arguments. Substantial evidence of personal interpretation, synthesis and evaluation. All major points covered. Excellent organisation and presentation for an undergraduate. Referencing correct. No (or only minor) errors in spelling and/or grammar.	From 50% upwards, work will show an increasingly **thorough** understanding of the literature and of concepts, analysis and use of a variety of sources, evaluation of theories and experience. Work will demonstrate a capacity for reasoned argument and judgement.
2.1 (60–69%) Very good grasp of knowledge, with evidence of wide reading and/or research. Issues understood and interpreted intelligently. Major points covered. Well-organised and presented. Evidence of a personal interpretation and a coherent argument, involving analysis,	While these criteria are relevant to all levels of undergraduate work, clearly a first-year

synthesis and evaluation. Referencing largely correct. Occasional spelling and/or grammatical errors.

2.2 (50–59%)

Good grasp of knowledge involved. Evidence of reading and research. Issues understood. Presentation and organisation clear. Most points covered. Provides the evidence and reports views on it. In doing so provides a fairly coherent response to the task. Referencing generally correct. Occasional spelling and/or grammatical errors.

3rd (40–49%)

Provides evidence and reports views but does not clearly relate them to the task. Some major points not covered. Some evidence of organisation. Work is too factual and descriptive. Repeated errors in referencing. More than the occasional error in spelling and/or grammar.

Fail (26–39%)

Little evidence of reading and/or research. Little evidence of understanding. Insufficient or misinterpreted evidence and views. Disorganised. Work and material presented is largely irrelevant to task set. A few minor points covered. Major and many errors in referencing. Frequent spelling and/or grammatical errors.

Bad Fail (<25%)

Scarce or no evidence of reading and/or research. Very disorganised and unclear. Majority of material irrelevant to the task set. Misinterpreted evidence. No major or minor points covered. Major and many errors in referencing. Many spelling and/or grammatical errors.

student is not expected to have developed these academic skills to the same level as is expected from a final-year student.

Appendix 3

Specific Essay Marking Scheme (first year undergraduate essay)

This is the marking scheme we used for one of our set essays (see below) It isn't usually shown to students for fairly obvious reasons but we are sharing it here so you can see what kind of guidelines the markers will be working to. Actually this is in far more detail than most marking schemes but we do this because we have a team of markers and we want to make sure there is consistency across the entire team. You can see how clearly we have specified what students should be writing.

What is stress? What aspects of team working might increase and what aspects might decrease levels of stress?

40% (pass)	A definition from the text or perhaps NIBOSH – physiological effects. The stress process – e.g. Cummings and Cooper or Arnold Cooper and Robertson. Some attempt at applying the concepts to work. No marks given for personal views on how to relax or on the things that worry them. Some references provided, probably only to material in the set text.
50% (2.2)	Discussion with reference to at least one of: • Role ambiguity, boundary spanning, single role conflict, transitions, burnout – Beehr 1995 • Yerkes Dodson law, Type A Type B – Rosenman, Friedman & Strauss, 1964, Bortner 1969. Definition of team working (possibly Mohrman & Mohrman). Description of at least one of: • group think (Janis) • Belbin team role • Form Norm Storm Perform (Tuckman) • description of why this affects performance • leader, team members, deviate, outcast • functional and psychological reasons for group formation

	• indication of what these models/theories show which might be stressful and what might help reduce stress • references consistent, probably almost all from the set text.
60% (2.1)	Full definition of stress and why it is important to understand it. Full definition of features of team working. Applications of theory applied to teams. Examples of stress on students as a whole as well as self. Consistent references almost entirely in the Harvard format. Some reference to work outside the set text.
70% (1st)	Wide reference to theory possibly including reference to theories of motivation. In-depth understanding shown of the causes of stress and whether the various interventions might or might not work. Thoughtful reflection on possible causes of stress on students in general. All theories cited correctly including dates. Extensive use of references to published work and a number outside the set text. Has clear understanding of the theory and has consulted original text. Referencing in correct format throughout.
85% (1st)	An outstanding piece of work, answering the question (all parts) completely and then going beyond the question. All theories fully understood, correctly referenced, evidence of extensive use of material above and beyond the set text especially use of primary sources including journals. Clearly argued, exceptionally well written, all references correctly cited. The best piece of work you could imagine someone at this level being able to write.

Appendix 4

Masters Degree Example Marking Scheme

80% or more	Distinction	To achieve over 80%, students should have presented a piece of work which is virtually faultless covering all the points mentioned for 70%+ but also going well beyond the core set work, delivering thoroughly well-argued cases and even presenting original ideas.
70% or more	Distinction	Overall this is an excellent piece of work for a postgraduate with all relevant material presented coherently, arguments evidenced well from the literature and evidence that the student has gone beyond the core material set in the module. All referencing completely correct and writing style clear and concise.
60–69%*	Merit	Student has shown excellent understanding of the subject matter, has combined own knowledge into the answer which addresses the question set. Some omissions but the material presented is correct.
50–59%	Pass	Student shows signs that understand topic in general terms and has made reference to the main theoryin the field. May have omitted some important points and/or made someminor errors.
40–49%	Fail	Student has probably not answered the question set or has tried to do so with minimal reference to published theory. Student may have made major errors of understanding.

39 or less	Bad Fail	Students refer to little or no published work or theory. Perhaps the question set is not addressed and the writing may be poorly structured with many grammatical errors meaning it is difficult to understand. Probably very short in length with few if any references, which are likely to be in the incorrect format.

* Sometimes universities only award the Distinction level so there is only fail – pass – distinction on the certificate.

Appendix 5

Examples of Extracts From Essays

Let us look at a few examples of good and bad essays. For the sake of clarity you will not have to read through an entire essay here – there are complete examples in Appendix 6 and Appendix 7 – but we are giving you some examples in the form of paragraphs. It will clarify the difference between a good and a not so good or even bad piece.

Example A

Paragraph A is a rather good piece. Table A lists what could have been improved and what is good (a tick is good, a *x* means missing or bad).

Paragraph A

CIT examines specific interactions between service firm employees and customers that are especially satisfying or especially dissatisfying. This technique is useful to companies as it offers qualitative information which is defined purely from a consumer perspective and, most importantly, the consumer's own experience with the business as a whole; incorporating the product on offer, the buying procedure and the behaviour of company employees. There are huge benefits for organisations when using CIT as the company can use this information as an indicator of how well the business is performing and how its employees are behaving and reacting to potential customers and existing customers. This is a crucial element when looking at the service industry, particularly when dealing with intangible services (where the product/service cannot be seen, tasted, felt heard or smelt before purchase) the company will rely on a good reputation to sell its services as well as relying on well-informed and helpful employees to encourage and trust the service on offer. Therefore CIT can enable a company to delve into customer experiences and examine how well the business is performing as a whole. It could be suggested that CIT is particularly useful when the service provided is new and there is little information readily available as CIT offers in-depth, reliable information which is also very cheap to get a hold of. It could be suggested that CIT also offers businesses a chance to get to know its customers, particularly customers of differing cultures. This is as respondents share their perceptions, rather than provide answers to defined questions by researchers. CIT is most useful as it can provide information from many stages in the consumer process. For example, Pre Sales, Post Sales and Pre Consumption, Consumption and Post Consumption, this provides a complete overview of the entire experience and process and differing functions of a company. It could be said that CIT is useful as it takes the form of an informal audit from a consumer perspective, which if utilised properly the company can use this to improve its service and build better relationships with customers. However it could also be suggested that it is hard to amend a damaged reputation as consumers who have had dissatisfying experiences tend to express this through word of mouth, therefore CIT is good at indicating problems and achievements, but it may be too late for the company to act upon a damaged reputation, particularly when dealing with intangible services.

Table A

Item	Met standards?	Room for improvement
Statement of claim		
Definition of terms	✓	It is important that you define concepts. The concept of CIT is explained, but the essay fails to state what the abbreviation CIT means.
Coherency	✓	
Referencing	x	You need to reference everything.
Description		
Elaborated on topic		
Examples		
Discussion		

Example B

Paragraph B is a rather less good piece, based on the same topic as Example A but falling short of it. Table B lists what could have been improved and what is good (a tick is good, x means missing or bad).

Paragraph B

CIT, critical incident theory, can offer a qualitative insight into how the service a company is providing is being received by its customers, however it could prove too late for some companies as the damage to the brand's reputation may have already been detrimental. It can be helpful and save some money. In some circumstances it may even increase customer satisfaction, but then at other times it may not. It depends on how a company does it, really. It is really important to save money and know about customer satisfaction. Some would even argue that monitoring staff will help improve customer experiences in a shopping environment. Increased competition between service-based businesses and increased consumer power requires organisations to provide and promote a good service, whether the service is the product bought or an attachment to a tangible product. The quality of this service can prove prevalent to consumers in a decision making and purchasing process as it is most likely that the consumer will choose to transact with the best service offered. What I understand now is that successful business can come from not only saving money and monitoring but also from asking people about how they feel about their shopping experiences.

Table B

Item	Met standards?	Room for improvement
Statement of claim	x	It is not really stated what the paragraph is about.
Definition of terms	✓	
Coherency	x	There is no coherency. The author is all over the place, bringing in various aspects, leaving the reader wondering what the paragraph is really about.
Referencing	x	You need to reference everything.
Description	✓	

(Continued)

Table B (Continued)

Elaborated on topic	x	Due to the variety of topics introduced, elaboration was not a realistic possibility. Always make sure to stay on track, following a path leading the reader through your essay.
Examples	x	Not really, in particular when compared to Example A.
Discussion	x	This is also partly due to the variety of topics introduced. It prohibited the author from writing a good discussion.

Example C

Paragraph C is an excellent piece. Table C lists what could have been improved and what is good (a tick is good, x means missing or bad).

Paragraph C

Stress can be defined as 'the strain which occurs when there is a lack of ability to cope with the demand' (Fincham & Rhodes, 2005, p. 62). Due to more recent changes in organizational working, teams are becoming an increasingly significant aspect of company success. Many aspects of team working, however, lead to the development of stress and it is up to the individual, the team as a whole and the team leader to counteract any stress sources. One source of stress is likely to be a feeling of entrapment (Fincham & Rhodes, 2005), yet it is likely that a participative leadership style can act as a mediating variable here, reducing any outset or increase in stress (Fincham & Rhodes, 2005). There are other methods that allow team members to tackle stress. One important way to avoid stress is through 'direct action ... by role innovation' (Bunce & West, 1996; Janssen, 2000; Fincham & Rhodes, 2005, p. 81). This involves group members in adapting new skills that can improve work-related stress. Janssen (cited in Fincham & Rhodes, 2005, p. 82), for instance, believes that higher job demands can be tackled by group members through adapting their work behaviours and expanding their knowledge to overcome setbacks. This suggests that by members of the team seeking techniques that enable them to cope with large quantities of work, levels of stress may be decreased and adjustment to their work performance is likely to develop and maintain a more effective team.

Table C

Item	Met standards?	Room for improvement
Statement of claim	✓	
Definition of terms	✓	The concept of team could also have been explained.
Coherency	✓	
Referencing	✓	Almost everything is referenced correctly
Description	✓	
Elaborated on topic	✓	
Examples	✓	
Discussion	✓	

Example D

Paragraph D is a less good piece. Table D lists what could have been improved and what is good (a tick is good, x means missing or bad).

Paragraph D

Stress, in the UK, is the second most established cause of absenteeism. Stress has also largely been correlated to health with a score of .3. This reasonably modest correlation is said to be underestimated but it is known that it costs the UK economy as much as £4 billion. One definition of stress is that the environment is presenting a harmful experience to the individual, but that also depends on the individual. Type As are competitive, very mentally and physically alert, involved in various activities, have the desire to achieve unobtainable goals and have a need for recognition and promotion. Conversely Type Bs have less time urgency, are less hostile, less competitive and less confrontational (Fincham & Rhodes, 2005, p. 78–9). It is therefore unsurprising that Type As are more likely to become stressed and develop stress-related illnesses such as coronary heart disease. They are also less likely to perform and/or tolerate working as part of a team. So, dependent on the individual, a person may feel more or less stressed by the environment.

Table D

Item	Met standards?	Room for improvement
Statement of claim	✓	
Definition of terms	x	The definition of stress is more a definition of one of its causes rather than the concept itself.
Coherency	x	There is no coherency. The author is all over the place, bringing in various aspects, leaving the reader wondering what the paragraph is really about.
Referencing	x	References missing.
Description	✓	
Elaborated on topic	x	There is no real elaboration on the topic.
Examples	x	Not really, in particular when compared to Example A.
Discussion	x	This is not really a discussion, simply a brief statement.

Appendix 6

Examples of Complete Essays with Annotations

The following two examples are actual essays written by students on the first year undergraduate Introduction to Organisational Behaviour module at Aston Business School. The question was set in our Introduction to OB course at Aston Business School. These example essays are reproduced here with the permission of the students (thanks for letting us use your work!) The students both received very good marks for their essays and we are extremely grateful that they allowed us to use them as examples in this book. Even though they are good essays, there is always room for improvement (no essay is ever perfect) so some comments relate to how they could be done even better. They are reproduced here to give very detailed illustrations as to what is required. You could read them with the mindset of the marker and see what comments you would make before turning to the comments at the end of each essay.

One condition, though – you must not use these essays in your own work at all! Just use them as exemplars of the quality you are striving to reach.

Example 1   An individual's work achievement can be best predicted by measuring their intelligence. Discuss.[i]

There are many proposals as to the nature and determinability of an individual's intelligence, each of which can be associated slightly differently with the prediction of work achievement. According to Sternberg (1984), they can be broadly divided into two categories by distinguishing between implicit and explicit theories; explicit indicating a theory uses empirical methods to measure intelligence, whereas implicit theories rely on intuitive assumptions.[ii]

A key example of an explicit theory is that of Thurstone (1938), who defines intelligence according to seven different primary abilities or aptitudes. These have been contrived using factor-analytical techniques, and so encompass all aspects of a person's capacity to understand and react to the world around them. Deary (2000, p. 6) explains that there is a 'surprising and consistent empirical finding' that scores based on the different aspects of intelligence tend to correlate, and that this is due to a general factor or

'G'. 'G' has then been refined further into reasoning processes (Gf) and crys-tallised ability (Gc). It is 'G' which infiltrates our intellectual activity and determines our potential level of performance. Consequently, it would seem logical that an employee with a higher level of intelligence would have a greater capacity to achieve in the workplace, simply because they would have a higher generic level of comprehension.[iii]

This reasoning can also be applied to the work of Gardner (1999, p. 43), who developed the theory of intelligence being 'biopsychological potential'. Within this theory, Gardner (1999, p. 40)[iv] identified eight 'mental capaci-ties', in which every individual has a varying degree of competency. Measurements of each of these aspects of intelligence can be combined to identify the type of mind of the individual, and therefore their strengths and weaknesses. Furthermore, by identifying the optimum qualities for a worker in a particular job, this measure of intelligence could be used to pre-dict how well somebody can achieve if they fulfil their biopsychological potential. In fact, Herrnstein and Murray (1996, p. 51) have found evi-dence for 'cognitive partitioning' of the labour market. This implies a per-son's occupation is directly correlated to their IQ, with people who have higher IQ having more occupational status. This, they claim, will be repro-duced in future generations, as intelligence level is inherited, and may one day lead to a reinstallation of the 'caste system' but in relation to intelli-gence. If this is the case, the argument that intelligence can be used to pre-dict an individual's work achievement is not only supported but extended, as it would have ramifications on the entire labour market.[v]

In contrast to this, implicit theories look at shared cultural assumptions and their effect on the mindset of companies and their employees. In this indirect fashion, intelligence may have a more subtle effect on the work-ings of a business. Dweck (2002, p. 33) explains that the common reaction to an individual with a high IQ is to believe that 'things should just come naturally' to them and that they will automatically have the ability to achieve in the workplace. She continues, however, by expressing concern over the fact that once this mindset has been instilled it often leads to the assumption that employees do not need to put in as much effort in order to achieve results. This, moreover, actually causes them to underachieve, and suggests that the correlation between intelligence and work achievement may not be a positive one after all. An illustration of this is the firm Enron, whose corporate management team placed immense emphasis on recruiting employees with high intelligence levels.[vi] The belief published in the Enron Annual Report (2002), cited in Fincham et al. (2005) p. 94, that 'smart people make smart hires' led to its collapse, according to Gladwell (2002), also cited in Fincham et al. (2005) p. 94, because the workforce became overconfident in their decision making when in effect they lacked experience. Hence, again there is evidence that an individual's work achievement can be predicted by measuring their intelligence, but not in the customary sense.

Dweck extended her research to look at this relationship in terms of the way in which intelligence is perceived. Whereas researchers such as Herrnstein and Murray (1996) believe that a person's intelligence is predetermined and therefore cannot be altered by external variables, others such as Sternberg (1984) oppose this view. Sternberg theorises that intelligence is merely the term applied to the compilation of intellectual competences, which can therefore be added to over time. This disputes Herrnstein and Murray's idea of a cognitive partitioning of the workforce, as intelligence would be a dynamic variable and so impossible to generalise. Dweck's research looked at the differentiating mindsets between people who believe intelligence is fixed and those who believe it can be developed. She found that within students those who believed it was fixed were disinclined to engage in learning opportunities, whilst other students believed they would be able to advance and hone their skills. Subsequently, it is arguable that perception of intelligence defines an individual's work achievement, rather than intelligence itself.

Deary (2000) claims that assumptions based on intelligence cannot be deemed as valid as so little is actually known about intelligence. Consequently, there may be other areas concerned with work achievement where more is known and a better prediction can be made. In light of research by Dweck that intelligence is not fixed, it stands to reason that education may be a more sensible predictor of work achievement as it is designed to add to a person's professional abilities and aid personal development. Research by Universities UK (2007, p. 1) concludes in the existence of a 'knowledge-based economy', where graduates succeed to higher levels than those without a degree. This would seem to substantiate the importance of education as a prediction of work achievement. On the other hand, given that employers generally specify a minimum level of education for their applicants, it is possible the entire idea is socially constructed and once again it is not intelligence itself that is a predictor of work achievement but the conceptions of intelligence.

Nyborg and Jensen (2001) found that a person's education, occupation and income were all correlated with their G score, implying that many of these areas are interlinked and therefore education and intelligence may be equally proficient in predicting work achievement. It is also worthwhile mentioning that everybody has a different experience of the educational system, thus a person's experiences, both educational and professional, may also be an indicator of how well they will achieve in the future. Nevertheless, Spearman (1904) himself said that the most reliable method of measuring someone's level of 'G' is one that is 'uncontaminated by education', implying that an empirical intelligence assessment may be the most reliable prediction of work achievement, as there is still an element of an individual's capabilities that is intrinsic and unaltered by external influences.

It is reasonable that a person's natural individuality and personality play a part in their achievement at work, as measures of intelligence can only define biological ability, not the extent to which it is employed. Factors of personality, for example those identified in the psychological model the 'Big Five' (Raad, 2000), determine how suitable a particular person is to a job, according to the particular characteristics it requires and whether these match those of the individual.[vii] If an employee is unsuited to a certain profession, they are likely to exhibit 'harmful physical and emotional responses', according to the National Institute for Occupational Safety and Health (2002), which not only indicates that they may not be able to achieve their potential but that stress may cause their work achievement to be impaired. As a result, personality may be a better prediction of work achievement than intelligence, as it reflects more than just inherent ability. This concept can be extended to look at specific qualities a person may need for a certain role, for instance a managerial position where decisions have to be made. Janis (1989) identified five decision-making styles, so it is highly likely certain styles will be more suitable to certain job roles and may therefore determine how well an individual can achieve in this role. Another key quality that may be important to professional success is that of leadership. Trait Theory, developed by Stogdill (1974) and quoted in Fincham et al. (2005) p. 324, claims that 'some are born to lead, others merely manage', due to natural ability and the presence of certain personality traits. Along these lines, it may be a biological fact that some people cannot naturally yield power over other individuals and have to rely on authority and the voluntary compliance on the part of their subordinates. It is interesting, however, that one of the leadership qualities listed by Stogdill is that of intelligence, which suggests that even though other factors may be important, intelligence is still fundamental to the prediction of work achievement.

Regardless of whether a person has the ability to complete a certain task, whether they actually do it depends on their level of motivation and how satisfied they are in their job. Robbins (2001) defined motivation as 'the process that accounts for an individual's intensity, direction and persistence of effort towards attaining a goal', which indicates that motivation is a critical factor when considering a person's work achievement. Process theories attribute that which motivates a particular person to their individual cognitive processes, for example Vroom's (1964) theory that motivation is the product of valence, expectancy and instrumentality, each of which are subjectively valued.[viii] This would therefore support the idea that personality affects level of attainment, as individual likes and dislikes would affect somebody's level of motivation, particularly if their personal goals do not coincide with that of the business as a whole. Conversely, content theories, which believe everyone has the same set of motivators, look at this hypothesis in a slightly different way. Maslow's (1954) hierarchy of needs depicts a series of components required for motivation, ranging from lower-order physiological needs to higher-order psychological needs. It is necessary to satisfy one need before it is possible to progress to the next of a higher order. Consequently, a person's motivation may still be linked to elements in their environment, as is the presumption in process theories, but these would have the same effect on everyone and there would be no scope for personal interpretation of what is necessary for a productive working environment. Thus, motivation would be less linked with personality or intelligence and would be more of a generic factor, and therefore may constitute a less important predictor of an individual's work achievement.

Another aspect relating to productivity that is linked to the idea of a productive working environment is that of the culture of a business, either concerning tasks undertaken by groups of employees or simply the culture of the business itself.[ix] Duncan (1981) defines an organisation as consisting of 'interacting and interdependent individuals', and therefore the atmosphere of a workplace can be very influential on the individual and their progress within the business. The concept of 'systematic soldiering' (Willis et al., 1981, p. 53), where output was consciously and deliberately restricted by members of the workforce, is an example of how an individual's work achievement is limited by the objectives of those around them. On the other hand, Alderfer (1972) includes 'relatedness' in his three elements of motivation, indicating that good relationships with those around you can also be beneficial and can provide the state of mind in which you can achieve. Nevertheless, the presence of others around an individual is likely to affect the extent to which they achieve within the organisation.

On reflection, it would appear that an individual's work achievement is not only determined by the individual themselves but also by many aspects of their working environment. It is arguable that intelligence is the most important of these influences, as it defines the realms of a person's comprehension and therefore the limit of their progress in a professional hierarchy. Nevertheless, current theories on intelligence are so diverse that it is impossible to categorically state its correlation, if any, with work achievement. Therefore, it may be more accurate to suggest that intelligence can best predict the potential an individual has for work achievement, rather than its realisation. This is due to the fact that individuals do not always utilise their abilities, and therefore factors including stress and motivation may prove to be better indicators of their level of productivity in the workplace.[x]

It is also significant that neither 'work achievement' nor 'intelligence' themselves are empirical variables, and therefore their measurement relies on techniques such as factor-analysis.[xi] This makes the entire process of predicting work achievement using intelligence unreliable, and suggests that if work achievement needs to be estimated a better alternative to intelligence might be level of education, which is both quantifiable and closely related to intelligence. To conclude, intelligence is a useful tool in the prediction of work achievement, but it is by no means the best forecaster due to its limited scope and unreliability.[xii]

References[xiii]

Alderfer, C. (1972) *Existence, relatedness, & growth*. First Edition. New York: Free Press.

Deary, I.J. (2000) *Looking Down on Human Intelligence: From Psychometrics to the Brain*. First Edition. Oxford: Oxford University Press.

Duncan, W. J. (1981) *Organizational Behaviour*. First Edition. Boston: Houghton Mifflin.

Dweck, C. (2002) 'Beliefs that make smart people dumb', in R.J. (ed.) *Why Smart People Can Be So Stupid*. London: Yale University Press.

Fincham, R. and Rhodes, P. (2005) *Principles of Organisational Behaviour.* Fourth Edition. New York: Oxford University Press.

Gardner, H. (1999) *Intelligence Reframed: Multiple Intelligences for the Twenty-first Century.* First Edition. New York: Basic Books.

Herrnstein, R.J. and Murray, C. (1996) *The Bell Curve: Intelligence and Class Structure In American Life.* First Free Press Paperback Edition. New York: Free Press.

Janis, I.L. (1989) *Crucial Decisions.* First Edition. UK: Free Press.

Maslow, A.H. (1954) *Motivation and Personality.* First Edition. New York: Harper.

National Institute for Occupational Safety and Health (1999) 'Stress ... at Work'. *Publication No. 99–101.*

Nyborg, H. and Jensen, A.R. (2001) 'Occupation and income related to psychometric g'. *Intelligence 29*: 45–55.

Raad, B.D. (2000) *The Big Five Personality Factors.* First Edition. USA: Hogrefe and Huber Publishers.

Robbins, S.P., Millett, B., Cacioppe, R. and Waters-Marsh, T. (2001) *Organisational Behavior.* Third Edition. Australia: Pearson Education.

Spearman, C. (1904) 'General intelligence objectively determined and measured'. *American Journal of Psychology. 14*: 201–293.

Sternberg, R.J. (1984) *Beyond IQ: A Triarchic Theory of Human Intelligence.* First Edition. Cambridge: Cambridge University Press.

Thurstone, L.L. (1938) *Primary Mental Abilities.* First Edition. Chicago: University of Chicago Press.

Universities UK (2007) *Research Report: The Economic Benefits of a Degree.* London: Universities UK.

Vroom, V. (1964) *Work and Motivation.* First Edition. New York: Wiley.

Willis, P. And Aronowitz, S. (1981) *Learning to Labour: How Working Class Kids Get Working Class Jobs.* Morningside Edition. UK: Columbia University Press.

Annotations

[i] So this question is of the 'discuss' type so a brief word about what to include in your answer. There are two concepts in the question – intelligence and performance – so the first thing to think about is how you define those terms and show you understand them by summarising the key theory in *both* areas. Discuss does imply that you need to come to a conclusion so you should be prepared to explore first the concepts, then the links between them before concluding one way or the other. Actually it very rarely matters which way you decide to conclude so long as you justify your argument and present compelling evidence. The pitfall of a question like this is that it doesn't really suggest a clear structure – 'compare and contrast' for example shows you to first make comparisons then contrast. With 'discuss' you need to pay particular attention to how you plan the essay and more than ever don't just start writing.

[ii] This is of course the introduction and the essay opens clearly using a definition right away. A stern marker might suggest that the opening paragraph might also contain a short sentence describing what the essay is going to do.

[iii] The author is showing they understand the concept by explaining the key features of intelligence and has also shown in-depth research through the use of original sources for the references. A less good essay might just use references from a single textbook – you usually get extra marks for showing you have read

the original. It happens that in our first-year module we tell students that they can pass by only using the textbook but of course if students want to gain a better grade they need to go to the original sources just like this student has.

iv   Full referencing being used here again. In fact you don't have to give a page number except when you are making a direct quote. You would be unlikely to lose marks for this in first year undergraduate work but possibly a harsh marker at a more advanced level might do so. As we say in Chapter 6 on referencing, there are often local conventions on referencing which you need to check.

v   A very neat use of different published papers to make an argument.

vi   The use of this real-life example brings a focus and relevance to the research references used so far in the essay. Not only is the example relevant, it is referenced, meaning readers could go and look it up if they wanted.

vii   Actually we might take issue with this statement as it probably isn't quite true. However, the point is tangential to the main points in the essay so doesn't really cost the student marks.

viii   The topic of motivation is not specifically asked for in the question so it could be dangerous to introduce it in the essay – you only get marks for points which answer the question. However, in this case the link is made very clearly and the point is very well made. As a rule, only move on to topics which are tangential to the question once you are absolutely certain you have completely covered the material directly related to the question.

ix   One thing this student might work on is the inclusion of short statements which help the reader understand what is coming next. It is really helpful to the marker to know the structure of the essay's various sections – otherwise it can start to look like a list and the reader wonders how long it is going to go on for. By stating upfront something like 'we will now address the following four theories ...' or something similar, an indication of structure can be given.

x   This is the discussion section – no new references introduced here since this is where the evidence presented in the essay so far is evaluated.

xi   Actually we wonder if this is really strictly true since we have already seen that there are measures of these concepts/constructs. You perhaps couldn't get away with this on a postgraduate essay as your terminology needs to be much more careful, but for an undergraduate the point is a fair one and shows the student has at least some understanding of what factor analysis is – which is quite advanced for this level.

xii   So the 'discuss piece' has been addressed throughout the essay and brought to a conclusion.

xiii   For a first-year essay, this is an extremely comprehensive list of references. It shows the student has spent a lot of time tracking down the material needed for the essay and they are presented in the correct format.

Example 2   An individual's work achievement can be best predicted by measuring their intelligence. Discuss.

In today's business world, large organisations place much emphasis on the need to assess the intelligence of individuals and use this as a basis to determine their ability to perform professional and administrative roles.[i]

According to Charles Spearman (1904) intelligence can be categorised into six main components.[ii] These include generating accurate responses, using abstract thinking, adjusting to the environment, adapting to new situations, the capacity for knowledge and the ability to learn from experience.[iii]

Other theories of intelligence focused more on speed to measure intelligence i.e. 'pure speed' (the speed of an individual's response); 'choice speed' (an ability to make quick choices); 'speed of lexical access' (the time it takes for someone to recall from long-term memory) and 'speed of reasoning' (interpreting and calculating a series of complex numbers).[iv]

Spearman extended his research by introducing the theory that there was a link between two or more measures of ability and where his sampling had identified errors, this was because for example, of 'lapses in people's concentration or poor test questions'. He therefore proposed that the overall results of an intelligence test could be reflected by one 'underlying ability factor' named as the 'G factor'. Schmidt and Hunter (1998) endorsed Spearman's theory by suggesting that the G factor was the best predictor of an individual's future performance.

However, at the interview stage, a company needs to be able to determine which candidates are most suitable for the specific positions they have in mind although each position could require a different level of particular intelligence.[v] In this case, an overall G factor analysis would be insufficient to determine an individual's strengths of intelligence in specific areas particularly as some of these strengths may be key requirements for the role.

Research undertaken by Thurstone (1938) introduced 'seven primary abilities' (aptitudes) and these were able to provide more relevant information on the abilities of an individual, the relationship between each of the seven aptitudes and the overall G score. The principles behind Thurstone's theory are used today in the development of aptitude tests for recruitment interviews and help employers identify individuals with the right levels of intelligence for the roles.[vi]

Gardner (1999) challenged both Thurstone and Spearman's theories by suggesting that an individual's intelligence is determined by more social, hereditary and external interest factors. According to Gardner, an individual's intelligence reflects a combination of their personal development, upbringing and education. Gardner therefore expanded the concept of the G factor to incorporate his eight intelligences and suggested that it was more in a company's interest to identify an individual's capabilities in problem solving and decision making rather than to assess their pure intelligence.

However, not all companies[vii] subscribe to Gardner's theories and still prefer to measure intelligence through academic achievement and the assessment of aptitudes. Unfortunately, there have been a number of major corporate failures in the last few years and an analysis of these have emphasised the extent to which the intelligence of company executives has played a part in their downfall.

Gladwell (2002), challenged the statement Enron made in its 2002 report 'Enron has been and always will be the consummate innovator because of our extraordinary people ... that makes us Enron'. This showed that the company was following a common business premise defined by the phrase 'smart people make smart hires' and that it placed too much emphasis on recruiting academically intelligent managers. It preferred to recruit capable students as opposed to older people with more business knowledge and relevant experience.

The Enron experience provides a current-day example that challenges the theoretical relationship between the measurement of intelligence and the ability of an individual to achieve. Enron's eventual bankruptcy proved that its recruitment approach was flawed as it should have taken into consideration Gardner's theory and the need to assess individuals based on his eight intelligences.[viii]

Unfortunately, the challenge for recruiters today is that whilst they could use complex intelligence-measuring criteria, assess aptitudes and all-round intelligence in order to shortlist potential candidates, each individual is unique. The application of these intelligence-measuring assessments serves mainly to enable employers to measure unique individuals in a consistent way and whilst these techniques do help to shortlist candidates, other additional and more intuitive assessments need to be performed to obtain a closer understanding of how well an individual might perform based on their perceived intelligence.

Confirming that someone is intelligent does not necessarily confirm that an individual will be able to perform or be well suited to any role. Further analysis of the Enron situation revealed that staff were being poached from one department to another and this was common practice. Those that were being poached were the brightest, however little consideration was given as to whether those poached staff could actually perform their roles well.

According to Dweck (2002) intelligence is not fixed but is malleable and could be improved through training, further education and work experience enabling a company to improve an individual's all-round capabilities in their chosen role. This suggests that a company doesn't need to recruit individuals on the basis of intelligence alone and potentially those with the right mindset and ambition achieve equally well.

Motivation and job satisfaction also affect the ability of an individual to achieve in their work. Terkell (1972) described the factory workplace as a 'dirty, noisy and dangerous place'.[ix] He also assessed clerical work as having low job satisfaction because of the excessive clerical routines and the poor levels of pay. The workplace therefore has an important influence on motivation, job satisfaction and individual achievement. The importance of workplace conditions was also endorsed by Maslow (1954) who identified that in an unfavourable environment there was a greater sense of insecurity and this reflected in the behaviours and low level of work achievement.[x]

In a favourable environment individuals are more motivated to progress and realise their full potential. Maslow proposed his self-actualisation theory in which he analyses an individual's psychological growth in five stages. These comprise psychological needs (for food, warmth clothing and shelter); security needs (for safety and freedom from fear); social needs (for a supportive relationship with others); self-esteem needs (for recognition and self-belief) and self-actualisation needs (to enable an individual to develop their full potential). Maslow believed that individuals should be encouraged to succeed and realise their full potential and that companies should provide opportunities to enable this. According to Maslow's hierarchy of needs, progressing through the five levels of self-actualisation increases an individual's motivation and this ultimately improves work achievement.

Herzberg (1959) supported Maslow's theories and used them to extend his own theories by analysing the extent to which individuals achieve job satisfaction in the workplace and how this impacts their personal motivation. He did this using a two-factor motivation model, which contained five Motivator and five Hygiene factors and suggested that with the right balance of Motivational and Hygiene factors, an individual can achieve a high level of job satisfaction, motivation and achievement.

Herzberg's motivators focused on assessing the impact of giving people greater responsibility, recognising their work, promoting them into new roles, enabling them to achieve and encouraging a good work–life balance. He also identified five hygiene factors that were seen as potential demotivating factors or factors that could limit an individual's job satisfaction. These comprised supervision, income-earning opportunities, a poor work environment, a rigid company policy and problems with colleagues.

Victor Vroom (1964) proposed the theory that there was a link between effort and reward and that this determined the level of an individual's motivation. He also proposed that motivation and job satisfaction were based on an individual's abilities, their personality, their understanding of their role and the opportunities presented to them. He suggested that whilst a person might be well motivated in their job, they may be restricted from achieving by limitations in their own ability. Using his VIE theory (Valence, Instrumentality and Expectancy) in his research, he was able to calculate the level of job motivation by measuring effort and performance and their relationship with a company's reward structure. The greater the reward, the higher the job satisfaction and motivation, the higher the effort and achievement.

Whilst the VIE theory concentrates on expectancy and the link between effort, performance and results, the results themselves depending on whether they are positive or negative undoubtedly affect motivation. Computer systems today are able to analyse inputs, outputs and performance to the nth degree and provide companies with management information that enables them to both predict and assess results.

Guirdham (1995) suggests that where results are negative, care needs to be taken when providing feedback to employees as this could have a damaging effect on motivation. He suggests that the most effective types of feedback are couched in positive terms, are well timed, regular, focused on issues within the control of the individual, specific (with examples), about publicly observed behaviours and should be sensitive so as not to invoke confrontation. By using these techniques, Guirdham suggests that managers will get the best out of their staff and be able to remotivate them when achievements and results are poor.

Job satisfaction has also been analysed in relation to an employee's general well-being. Warr (2002) developed a two-dimensional model to capture an individual's attitude towards work and their strength of feeling. The model has three measurement axes to assess the job characteristics based on pleasure/displeasure, anxiety/comfort and enthusiasm/depression. This could provide an indication to employers as to an individual's potential to achieve.

The characteristics of a job also play an important part in determining an individual's job satisfaction. Hackman and Oldham (1975) developed a model that contains both the content and process models of motivation but also explains an individual's need and expectancies. They identified five core dimensions which are 'skill variety' (skills and talents required); 'task identity' (an identifiable objective); 'task significance' (the importance of the task to the organisation); 'autonomy' (the ability to make decisions) and 'task feedback' (the provision of information on the effectiveness of performance).

According to Hackman and Oldham if these core dimensions exist in a job, an individual will experience three critical psychological states. These states are 'experienced meaningfulness of work, experienced responsibility for work outcomes and knowledge of results of work activities' and when they are all experienced by an individual their job satisfaction, motivation and achievement will be high.[xi]

Job satisfaction clearly plays an important part in determining the motivation of individuals and companies need to ensure they understand the characteristics of each role in order to monitor and predict an employee's behaviour and achievement.

Research in this sphere in the last two centuries has been extensive and reflects the thirst for a greater understanding of what drives an individual's achievement.[xii] Some of this interest has also come from the world of business where companies are seeking to find better ways of improving an individual's performance as, the greater the achievement of individuals, the greater the performance of the company. In certain sectors of business, i.e. manufacturing, the achievement of individuals can have a considerable bearing on the output and profits of the company.

Various theorists have demonstrated a link between job satisfaction and personal motivation. Therefore, before advertising for vacancies and setting the minimum level of intelligence required, companies need to ensure they understand the motivator and hygiene factors involved. Clearly the Enron approach to recruitment was inappropriate and proved that intelligence was not the best predictor of achievement.

Every role requires a certain degree of intelligence, however, the balance between intelligence, skill and experience needs to be considered. This is important in the selection of the right candidate for the role and demonstrates that intelligence should not be the only consideration.

However, once a candidate has been appointed to the role, an individual's achievement is best determined by job satisfaction and motivational factors and these need to be reviewed on a regular basis in order to identify fluctuations (particularly negative ones) and allow the company and the individual to improve the position and the individual's level of achievement.

Bibliography[xiii]

Fincham, R. and Rhodes, P. (2005) 'Principles of Organisational Behaviour'. Fourth Edition. Oxford University Press, New York, USA.

Secondary references

Spearman, C. (1904) 'General intelligence objectively determined and measured', *American Journal of Psychology*, New York, USA.
Cited in: 'Principles of Organisational Behaviour' (Fourth Edition)
Schmidt, F.L. and Hunter, J.E. (1998) 'The Validity and Utility of Selection Methods in Personnel Psychology: Practical and Theoretical Implications of 85 Years of Research Findings', *Psychological Bulletin*.
Cited in: 'Principles of Organisational Behaviour' (Fourth Edition)
Thurstone, L.L. (1938) 'Primary Mental Abilities', University of Chicago Press, Chicago, USA.
Cited in: 'Principles of Organisational Behaviour' (Fourth Edition)
Gardner, H. (1999) 'Intelligence Reframed: Multiple Intelligences for the Twenty-First Century', Basic Books, New York, USA.
Cited in: 'Principles of Organisational Behaviour' (Fourth Edition)
Gladwell, M. (2002) 'The talent myth', *The Times*, UK.
Cited in: 'Principles of Organisational Behaviour' (Fourth Edition)
Dweck, C. (2002) 'Beliefs that make smart people dumb', Yale University Press, London, UK.
Cited in: 'Principles of Organisational Behaviour' (Fourth Edition)
Terkell, S. (1972) 'Working', Avon, New York, USA.
Cited in: 'Principles of Organisational Behaviour' (Fourth Edition)
Maslow, A.H. (1943) 'A theory of human motivation', *Psychological Review*.
Cited in: 'Principles of Organisational Behaviour' (Fourth Edition)
Herzberg, F. (1966) 'Work and the Nature of Man', World Press, Cleveland.
Cited in: 'Principles of Organisational Behaviour' (Fourth Edition)
Vroom, V.H. (1964) 'Work and Motivation', Wiley, New York, USA.
Cited in: 'Principles of Organisational Behaviour' (Fourth Edition)
Guirdham, M. (1995) 'Interpersonal Skills at Work' (Second Edition), Prentice Hall, London, UK.
Cited in: 'Principles of Organisational Behaviour' (Fourth Edition)
Warr, P.B. (2002) 'The study of well-being, behaviour and attitudes' in 'Psychology at Work', Penguin Books, London, UK.
Cited in: 'Principles of Organisational Behaviour' (Fourth Edition)
Hackman, J.R. and Oldham, G.R. (1975) 'Development of the job diagnostic survey', *Journal of Applied Psychology*.
Cited in: 'Principles of Organisational Behaviour' (Fourth Edition)

Annotations

[i] The first sentence is a little bland – do organisations really do this? We don't know if we agree. One sage piece of advice is to go back over your essay and delete the first sentence or paragraph you write. Often it is only really being used to get yourself going – this is a good example of this. This is actually going to be a great essay but the first sentence doesn't really show us this.

ii   It would have probably been better to use a colon then list the six items. We are being *very* picky though!

iii   Having listed these, it would probably have been better to briefly describe what they are and/or to critique how they were derived. The former is easy, the latter would be a student going for an exceptionally high mark.

iv   This is a good point but loses a lot of its impact by not citing examples and sources. It isn't a case of plagiarism by any means though since the student is not in any way trying to pass the ideas off as her own.

v   This has been a reasonable opening to the essay but the student seems to have now changed from mentioning intelligence theory into the interview process. It would probably have been better to first cover all the theory then move to applying it to the workplace. The question is in two parts (predicting work achievement and intelligence measurement) and it is a good idea to deal with the second part of the question first in this case but perhaps the student has jumped off into the other part of the question too early.

vi   Now the structure of the essay is becoming clear – each theory of intelligence is being applied to the issue of work performance. It would have probably helped us (the readers) if this had been set out in the first paragraph. We call this 'signposting' where the writer tells the readers what is going to happen in the essay. It is often a very small piece of work to do this – a matter of a few words – but makes the reading of the essay so much easier – and doing this well will almost certainly lead to higher marks.

vii   Companies aren't people so can't really subscribe or not to theory. Of course the student means the decision makers in businesses meaning probably HR people. In fact we would doubt many HR people will know (or remember) these theories but perhaps this is a side issue. To be fair, this is a linking passage and the link to the next section is made and the point it links to about Enron is a good one.

viii   Perhaps we are being picky again but of course the problem at Enron wasn't only to do with poorly performing people, it was to do with fraud. Of course intelligence isn't related to morality or ethics (people can be clever and bad, not clever and good!) and so intelligence testing doesn't help in this way. Perhaps the student might have said this directly – it is inferred but not actually stated.

ix   For a direct quote, you need to put the page number as well as the author and date.

x   It is a good idea to include motivation in this essay even though it is not directly asked for in the question. This is because obviously some people work harder than others and this is independent of intelligence measures. However, a short sentence saying that this is where the essay is going would have helped enormously.

xi   This is an area where the student is scoring very good marks. This theory was not included in the lecture for the module so it is something she has brought in from her own reading. It is also really very relevant to the question (and makes us wonder if we should have included the topic in the lectures!)

xii   You probably need to justify statements like this – how are you able to say there has been a lot of research and compared to what?

xiii   The references are generally in the right format but there is no need to separate out the list like this. Just put the title References and then list them alphabetically for the Harvard system. For Chicago, numerical order of course.

Appendix 7

Example of a Fictitious Essay with Annotations

The following essay was not written by the students who kindly contributed their excellent essays for use in this book. It is a fictitious piece of work written by us based on our experience of the sorts of mistakes students made when writing this essay. It shows some of the common pitfalls we have seen over the years. Do not take this final example as something to aim for as it is deliberately shown as a poor piece of work!

An individual's work achievement can be best predicted by measuring their intelligence. Discuss.

Intelligence can be understand as the ability when people see a problem, then solve the problem. For quite a long period of time, Intelligence Quotient had been used as the most essential standard to test whether a person is intelligent or not. Lots of organizations recognized that an individual's work achievement can be predicted from an intelligence test score.[i]

But in general, it is extremely difficult to make precise definitions as to what intelligence is. We might say that some students have a 'high IQ' and that these students get good grades at university but we cannot be sure that they will be successful after they graduate.[ii] On the other hand, many famous people were not very good at studying when they were students or have been reported as being told they had low intelligence and yet were still able to be successful. These facts[iii] conflict with the view that an individual's work achievement can be predicted from an intelligence test score.[iv]

An increasing number of scholars have focused on how to make a precise determination as to what intelligence is. For example Peter Salovey and John D. Mayer's theory about 'emotional intelligence' (1990) and Howard Gardner's 'Multiple Intelligences' (1999).[v]

Gardner's theory challenges the traditional view of intelligence.[vi] He argued that there exists a multitude of intelligences, and quite independent of each other; that each intelligence has its own strengths and constraints (Fincham & Rhodes, 2005. P140–P142)[vii]

This method recognizes that we learn, we communicate and we solve problems in eight ways which we can understand as linguistic; logical mathematical; musical; bodily (kinaesthetic); spatial; interpersonal;

intrapersonal (the ability to understand oneself); naturalistic (the ability to recognize, name and classify) (Fincham & Rhodes, 2005. P142)[viii] that is, each individual has a unique mixture of eight intelligences. This is totally different from the traditional way to measure intelligence which just measures the ability in one or two areas. Because in the traditional way, the questions of the test are just seeing about the abilities of logical mathematical intelligence and linguistic intelligence. And both of them are very important abilities for study, so this can explain why the students' academic education could be predicted from the score on the traditional intelligence test. But it is not suitable for measuring an individual's work achievement, there are many factors that can affect one person's work achievement, but the traditional intelligence test just mentions a little factors. At work, Gardner suggests it would be more useful to find out about someone's favoured way of thinking and solving problems, and then make decisions about hiring and training (Fincham & Rhodes, 2005. P142) For example, accountants should pay attention to a form of logical mathematical intelligence, and perhaps marketing specialists should draw on more instinctive intelligence in order to be able to see trends and predict which products will sell best.

The concept of emotional intelligence was developed by Peter Salovey and John D. Mayer (1990) who argued that the traditional concept of intelligence ignores the emotional competency (Huczynski & Buchanan, 2007. P146). Emotional intelligence is defined as being 'The ability to perceive emotion, integrate emotion to facilitate thought, understand emotions, and to regulate emotions to promote personal growth'.[ix] The ability-based model views emotions as useful sources of information that help one to make sense of and navigate the social environment. The model proposes that individuals vary in their ability to process information of an emotional nature and in their ability to relate emotional processing to a wider cognition. This ability is seen to manifest itself in certain adaptive behaviors.[x]

Emotional intelligence[xi] is the ability to identify, integrate, understand and reflectively manage our own and other people's feelings. The emotional intelligence involves five main dimensions. Self-awareness is the ability to recognize and understand your mind, your emotions; Regulating feelings is the ability to control your emotions, and to think before acting; Motivation is a passion to work for reasons; Empathy is the ability to recognize and understand other people's emotions; Social skills are the abilities to manage the relationships and build networks (Huczynski & Buchanan, 2007. P147). These dimensions of emotional intelligence are summed up by Daniel Goleman (1998), who recognizes that emotional intelligence is more important to career success than the traditional concept of intelligence[xii] and so a number of organizations now pay more attention to improve emotional intelligence in management. As we have already mentioned, there are many factors can affect one person's work achievement. Some scholars said that emotional intelligence is too broadly defined and the definitions are unstable. One of them, Woodruffe (2001) argues that emotional intelligence's contribution to job performance has been exaggerated (Huczynski & Buchanan, 2007. P149).[xiii]

Overall, if the person contains great ability no matter from multiple intelligences and emotional intelligence, the contribution to job performance would be increased and improved from these factors.

An individual's work achievement also may be affected by the job's motivations. Motivation occurs when people do something because they want to do it, and also it is the will to work. This comes from the enjoyment of the work itself or from the desire to achieve certain goals e.g. earn more money or achieve promotion. Generally, the higher the motivation is, the better the performance achieved. So managers spend lots of time working out how best to motivate their workers and there are number of different opinions about how this can be best done.

From Maslow's theory, we can know that he believes everyone has different needs, and all of them can be organized as a hierarchy. There are five levels of human needs which employees need to achieve at work. At the base of the hierarchy are physical needs such as food and bed. Only once they achieved a lower level of need, then the worker would be motivated by the next level of need. Instead of physical needs, people become motivated to achieve needs such as security and protection. Also, from the work they do, they want to know more people, and make friends, which is known as their social needs. In addition, people may work for their self-esteem so are rewarded not only in terms of salary but also in terms of status and the esteem other people hold them in.[xiv]

From the above, it can be seen that a business should offer different incentives to workers in order to help them achieve their different needs. The managers should also recognize that all the workers are not motivated by earning more and more money, because different people have different degrees of need.[xv]

Hertzberg's theory is close with Maslow's and he believes in a two-factor theory of motivation. From his research, he found that there were certain factors that would directly motivate employees to work harder, and these factors he called Motivators. However there were also some factors that would demotivate an employee to work harder, and these he called Hygiene factors. Motivators are more concerned with the job itself. For instance how interesting the work is and achievement, recognition and promotion, so the motivators can create positive satisfaction. Hygiene factors are factors which 'surround the job' rather than the job itself, like company policy, the interpersonal relations and working conditions, so hygiene factors can create job dissatisfaction (Ian Marcouse, 2003, P222)[xvi]

In conclusion, for the students, their 'academic' education could be predicted from the score on an intelligence test, but at work, the score of intelligence tests seems not the decisive element in predicting workers' job performances.[xvii] Generally, multiple intelligences and emotional intelligence are more useful than traditional intelligence in job performance. Most jobs change over time, so predictions based on current measures are unreliable (Huczynski & Buchanan, 2007. P165) For an individual, the personality is also a very important factor, influencing the work achievement. People are all different, and different people have different personality. So the company should use the employee whose personality matches

the personality required for the occupation. An individual's work achieve-
ment also may be affected by the motivations, but there is no one method
can be the best way to motivate employees, and there is no one method
suitable for all situations. Because everyone is different, and job perfor-
mance usually depends on many factors.

Bibliography^{xviii}

Robin Fincham & Peter Rhodes, (2005) *Principles of Organizational Behaviour* (Fourth edition) Oxford: Oxford University Press.

Andrzej A. Huczynski & David A. Buchanan, (2007) *Organizational Behaviour (sixth edition)* London: Pearson Education Limited.

Jak Jabes, (1978) *Individual processes in Organizational Behaviour,* Illinois: AHM Publishing Corporation.

Ian Marcouse, (2003) *Business Studies (second edition),* London: Hodder Arnold.

Mike Smith, (1991) Analysing *Organizational Behaviour,* London: The MACMIL-LAN PRESS LTD.

Nancy Wall, (2003) *A–Z economics and business studies Handbook (3rd editon),* London: Hodder Arnold.

Annotations

ⁱ   This looks like something the student has made up off the top of his head. In fact there is some truth in this, not least because it is a summary of something written in the textbook. The paragraph therefore shows a lack of understanding (it is badly written but it is just about possible to work out what the student had in mind) and there is no reference to the text so the student is immediately in danger of being accused of plagiarism. It is probably not the worst sort of plagiarism, where the student has been deliberately cheating, but still shows he hasn't understood how to cite references so this essay is on the road to failure from the start.

ⁱⁱ   This is a very good point and absolutely correct. However, it is not evidenced in any way so doesn't count towards the mark.

ⁱⁱⁱ   Perhaps overcooking this to call these anecdotes facts. So far as an essay is concerned, a fact is something which you can corroborate with evidence from the literature. To be honest, there is a whole debate about whether there are any real facts in social science – only perceptions. But perhaps this is going too far!

^{iv}   We haven't established whether anyone really has this view. The question merely asks to you discuss the assertion. No evidence has been presented which would indicate that anyone thinks intelligence is a useful predictor of performance.

^v   Now this does look promising. These are indeed two great theories to work on, so we are now looking forward to the student getting into his stride ...

^{vi}   What has happened? The student raised the idea of EQ first in the previous paragraph so we are expecting something about this now. However, they have jumped on to Gardner. Perhaps we are going to return to EQ later ...

^{vii}   Aha – a reference. It isn't quite in the right format as you don't use page numbers when citing a general point – only when using a direct quote. It isn't so bad an infringement though and it is a relief to see some references being used.

^{viii}   A good quotation – although the quoted words should be in inverted commas and the eagle-eyed reader will note the slightly incorrect format. However, the problem here is that the student has not explained what these things mean. The student in the last essay did something similar, but given the quality of

the rest of this essay we are not at all convinced this student actually knows what all these mean. So, yes the quote is referenced so the student is not suspected of plagiarism here but we need to be convinced he understands what he has just written.

ix   This is a reasonable definition but is not the student's own. A quick look on the Internet confirms that it was downloaded from Wikipedia – by the way, NEVER EVER use material from Wikipedia in essays! There is no guarantee at all that the person writing it is right and there is a vast amount of good, scientific literature for you to use.

x   Now this is plagiarism. The student has copied this (again from Wikipedia) and is passing it off as his own. To be honest, it doesn't add at all to the essay and this sort of thing really stands out to the reader as it doesn't fit and is written in a different style from the rest of the essay. Even if the reader didn't realise it was stolen from somewhere else, it simply does not add to the essay at all. Our interpretation at this point is that the student is desperate – either not understanding the work or having left it too late to do the necessary preparation work.

xi   Aha! Now we have emotional intelligence. The student just hasn't laid out the structure logically. He has lost some marks for this but, if the next section is well researched, he could still be OK.

xii   Incidentally this is questioned by a number of recent studies which show a lack of evidence for Goleman's claims. His book (emotional intelligence) is a bestseller and has made him very rich. It doesn't, however, mean to say he is right! It is fine to mention the book and indeed because it is so popular it would seem odd to omit it, but you must be critical and question if there is evidence for the claims. In this case, we suspect the student has not actually read Goleman, still less the critical papers.

xiii   It is great to report the critics but we simply aren't convinced that the student has really understood what these criticisms are.

xiv   Students seem fond of trotting out an explanation of Maslow which does become tedious to the marker. However, there is some merit in its inclusion here although the student has missed out self-actualisation but the rest is about right. The key problem here is a lack of reference though so almost no marks are awarded for this section.

xv   This seems good advice but not really part of this essay as the task set is to evaluate the effectiveness of using intelligence tests to predict performance, not to discuss how to motivate workers.

xvi   This is a bit of a giveaway. The book referenced here is an A-level textbook for business studies. It is doubtless a useful book for its purpose but it is not suitable to use as reference material for a degree. It indicates to us that the student is probably using material (or even a complete essay) used at A level which is almost certain to fall short of the standards required for university. By all means use different books if you can't understand the material in the one you have been set as reading, but you should then go on to try to understand what the set text is saying and work from this.

xvii   Actually this is quite a good point but not fully covered in the essay. Frequently students include new ideas in the conclusion and this is a bad thing. The conclusion should just pull together points you have made elsewhere and come to a full stop. If you have been asked to come down for or against something, this is where it is done.

xviii The list of references isn't too bad. The student has included some references which aren't used in the text and some of the formatting isn't quite right (as you will have noticed I'm sure!) We would suggest the list is headed references not bibliography.

Index

Research Methods Books from SAGE

Basics of QUALITATIVE RESEARCH 3e

Juliet Corbin
Anselm Strauss

The Mixed Methods Reader

Vicki L. Plano Clark ■ John W. Creswell

DOING QUALITATIVE RESEARCH USING YOUR COMPUTER

A PRACTICAL GUIDE

CHRIS HAHN

SECOND EDITION
INTERVIEWS
Learning the Craft of Qualitative Research Interviewing

Steinar Kvale
Svend Brinkmann

DISCOVERING STATISTICS USING SPSS THIRD EDITION

ANDY FIELD

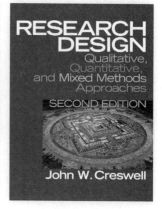

RESEARCH DESIGN
Qualitative, Quantitative, and Mixed Methods Approaches
SECOND EDITION

John W. Creswell

www.sagepub.co.uk